This Is My Body

This Is My Body

*Philosophical Reflections on Embodiment
in a Wesleyan Spirit*

Edited by
JOHN THOMAS BRITTINGHAM
and CHRISTINA M. SMERICK

Foreword by Jeffrey Bloechl

☞PICKWICK *Publications* · Eugene, Oregon

THIS IS MY BODY
Philosophical Reflections on Embodiment in a Wesleyan Spirit

Pickwick Publications
An Imprint of Wipf and Stock Publishers
199 W. 8th Ave., Suite 3
Eugene, OR 97401

www.wipfandstock.com

PAPERBACK ISBN 13: 978-1-4982-0792-8
HARDCOVER ISBN 13: 978-1-4982-0794-2

Cataloguing-in-Publication Data

This is my body : philosophical reflections on embodiment in a Wesleyan spirit / edited by John Thomas Brittingham and Christina M. Smerick ; foreword by Jeffrey Bloechl.

xii + 164 p. ; 23 cm. Includes bibliographical references and index.

ISBN: 978-1-4982-0792-8 (paperback) | ISBN: 978-1-4982-0794-2 (hardback)

1. Human body. 2. Human body—Religious aspects. 3. Wesley, John, 1703–1791. 4. Theology, Doctrinal. I. Bloechl, Jeffrey, 1966–. II. Brittingham, John Thomas. III. Smerick, Christina M. IV. Title.

BT741.3 .T53 2016

Manufactured in the U.S.A.   02/19/2016

Contents

Church Bodies

Altered Bodies

Contributors

John M. Bechtold, PhD candidate at Iliff School of Theology, University of Denver

Matthew Bernico, PhD candidate at the European Graduate School

John Thomas Brittingham, PhD, Instructor of Philosophy, Greenville College

Amanda DiMiele, MDiv candidate, Duke Divinity School

Brannon Hancock, Assistant Professor of Practical Theology and Christian Ministry, Indiana Wesleyan University

Jonathan Heaps, PhD candidate, Marquette University

Craig Keen, Professor of Theology and Philosophy, Azusa Pacific University

Joyce Ann Konigsberg, PhD candidate, Dusquene University

Michael Lodahl, Professor of Constructive Theology, Point Loma Nazarene University

Teri Merrick, Chair and Professor of Theology and Philosophy, Azusa Pacific University

Eric Severson, PhD, adjunct professor, Seattle Pacific University and Seattle University

Christina M. Smerick, PhD, Chair and Associate Professor of Philosophy and Religion, Greenville College

Foreword

CHRISTIANS CANNOT LONG TURN their eyes away from the Cross, and any attempt to identify with the crucified God-Man comes soon enough to the fact that the path to redemption calls upon the entirety of one's being—soul, to be sure, but also body. If "path" and "journey" are primary metaphors in human consciousness, this is because human beings find themselves in terrain that is as assuredly physical as it is mental and spiritual. A basic fact of our condition emanates from the Cross: one is embodied. One is flesh animated by soul, and soul that is enfleshed. Wishing not to decide in favor of either of the two, as if one comes before the other, Gregory of Nyssa considered that the soul and the body are created together and at the same time. In the former, there is the principle of a being capable for growing closer to the divine. In the latter, of course is the principle of our limitation. We are bound to the earth, engaged with the things of this life, even as we are also elevated toward God. This no doubt opens the way for much that can be said about the origin, by which an infinite being supports a relation with finite beings. But it also suspends a riddle over the mystery of the end, by which the distance between finite and infinite would be overcome. What becomes of this body that I am when I am no longer of this world? The question of the body troubles the doctrine of Resurrection, as Paul learned in his encounter with the Athenians.

If we may thus assure ourselves that Christianity is necessarily a religion of the body, this hardly determines quite how or even to what degree Christians might address themselves to the theme. Even if we suppose that it is created simultaneously with the soul, there is still the question of the relation between the two substances. Augustine sometimes proposes the image of marriage between the two. It has been a tendency of the Scholastics to start from an irreducible unity in which the animated body cannot be mere matter and in which the incarnated soul cannot be pure spirit. There is no single and simple reason for how it is that some modern theologians have gone away from these conceptions toward a more dualistic understanding. A few well–known developments suggest a direction for further reflection. One easily surmises, for example, that as the new science of the sixteenth and seventeenth centuries claimed increasing authority in study of the body, physical processes and natural laws, theologians were strongly tempted, or even felt compelled, to minimize their own references to a body whose movements are intelligible according to the presence of a soul. And it is well known that some pietism responds directly to this challenge by taking some distance not only from the new sciences but also their subject matter.

Perhaps these few remarks can serve as a lens through which to study the present collection of essays on the theme of embodiment in a modern theologian whose relation with the modern world can fairly be described as tense and undecided. Does John Wesley offer us a theology of the body? The contributing authors suggest not, or at any rate agree that what of it that one finds in his writings falls short of what one would like. Interestingly, they propose not to take Wesley back to Augustine or Nyssa, but instead forward to what has been learned about body and embodiment after Wesley and indeed down to our own time. I will attempt neither a summary of their efforts nor even an overview of the collected essays. Instead, I wish only to note two complications that enrich their work. First, it must not be forgotten that what are variously called philosophies of the body, corporeality, and flesh belong either to the turn to the subject that dominates much of European thought from Descartes through Husserl, or else to a subsequent turn to decenter the subject. Wesley's thinking does not appear centered on an autonomous subject, and it is not evident that the discovery of heteronomy in late twentieth century philosophy (e.g., Emmanuel Levinas, Jean-Luc Marion) is quite the heteronomy of most Christian theology. A number of essays collected here do situate themselves in the field of this question.

Second, it also should be kept in mind, and submitted to close scrutiny, that a good deal of contemporary philosophy comes rather late to prolonged attention on the theme of embodiment. Whether one favors Merleau-Ponty's remarkable persistence with the phenomenality of body and flesh, or the emancipatory potential of neo-Nietzschean efforts to welcome drive and life into our account of desiring bodies, this means that any number of factors defining a perspective will have been settled before thinking has come precisely to the body. It seems unlikely—certainly with regard to the two cases that I have just mentioned—that what has been settled in recent philosophy at all matches what Wesley will have considered settled. This, too, marks a field in which one might read with come profit several of the essays gathered here.

These few complications are recorded only in the margins of a project that comes down to nothing less than early movement toward the massive updating of canoncial texts. Does all of this call for considerably more work? Undoubtedly. But it is the merit of this volume to have brought them to light, and indeed to have made that additional work appear much needed.

—Jeffrey Bloechl,
Boston College

INTRODUCTION

The Body as Problematic, the Body as Theme

John Thomas Brittingham and Christina M. Smerick

WHETHER YOU LIKE IT or not, you have a body. In spite of my best efforts and against my better judgment, I have a body too. No amount of meditative contemplation, Sermon on the Mount inspired divestment of the flesh, and hallucinatory recreational activities can get rid of the fact that, at the end of the day, you and I will still be bodies. Whether we treat them as sagging bags of flesh we carry around with us or as finely tuned locomotive machines, our bodies are not going anywhere without us. For better and for worse, we are our bodies.

Yet both Western philosophy and theology have struggled with bodies. Both disciplines have ignored, mortified, demonized and sanitized the flesh, or, at best, they have prioritized the soul, spirit and/or mind over against the flesh. The intertwining of these disciplines throughout Western history has created a feedback loop, a reification of Platonism's dichotomy down through the ages, terminating only in modernity. Even the separation of philosophy from theology, however, did not produce on either side a more positive account of the body. Rather, while going their separate ways, both disciplines continued their emphasis upon the mental over the physical. It is only at the turn of the twentieth century that we find Western philosophy orienting itself toward bodies as sites for investigation.

That the body is a fact of existing in the world does not make the body philosophically interesting. What makes the body philosophically interesting and worthy of investigation is that our relationship to the body is paradoxical from the very start. In this sense, the body is similar to Martin Heidegger's description of the relationship between Being and Dasein in *Being and Time*: The body is that which is closest to us and therefore extremely difficult to see. You might respond to this Heideggerian formulation of the body problem by saying that we can appeal to anatomy, biology, and physiology. We can understand how every ligament and sinew functions and we can see how the different parts of the body stretch and contract to create movement. We can see all the parts of the body and how they fit together like a finely tuned machine. However, that the body is close to us while being difficult to observe is not the paradox of the body. The mechanistic approach to the body is not intelligible without recourse to the body in the first place. You cannot look at an x-ray of the body without using your eyes, which are, it turns out, a part of the body. Thus, the paradox of the body is that we must use our body to understand our body.

The body is both that which can be looked at as other than ourselves and yet always a part of ourselves. Such a paradox, one must admit, is quite philosophically interesting. How philosophy has explored the body is another matter entirely. While there are many methods we could employ to examine the body from a philosophical standpoint, it is something of a rarity in the history of Western philosophy. Indeed, as we will see, in the history of Western thought, taking the body seriously is a relatively recent development.

A HISTORY OF THE PHILOSOPHY OF THE BODY

The customary place to begin with a history of philosophy's treatment of the body is with the beginnings of philosophy itself. That is, we begin with Plato.[1] Long seen as the father or at least one of the fathers of philosophy, Plato's works continue to loom large over the two thousand plus year history of the practice of philosophy. Yet, one cannot talk about Plato and his main character Socrates without mentioning that it is a *certain Plato* and a

1. This is not to say that Plato is the first philosopher. Rather, this is to say that, for much of what constitutes Western Philosophy, Plato is the first philosopher.

certain Socrates one talks about. There is no one interpretation of Plato to rule them all, as is the case with the rest of the Western canon, but several thematics of Plato's work figure in just about any and all interpretations of his work.

For much of Western history, Plato has been characterized as an idealist, a kind of proto-Cartesian. As the so-called "Theory of the Forms" found in *The Republic* makes clear, there is a split between sensible, imperfect knowledge and perfect, intelligible knowledge.[2] Such a split extends beyond the confines of epistemological and metaphysical speculation to the area of life itself. The body, for all its persistence in lived experience, is seen as secondary and negative compared to the perfection that is the intelligible world of the forms. The body is the seat of the drives, of those parts of the soul one ought to starve whereas the intelligible parts of the soul ought be fed through contemplation and dialectic.

However, this dualistic structure—between sensible body and intelligible intellect—is not absolute. It is an anachronism to read Plato's metaphysics as being so disconnected or opposed to one another that body and mind constitute separate entities. In fact, to read the "Theory of the Forms" section of *Republic* carefully is to note that all sections of the "divided line" participate in one another.[3] That is, every way of knowing and every object known, whether sensible or intelligible, participate somewhat in that which is higher or "better" known. Accordingly, even the images that Plato locates at the bottom of the divided line reflect the perfection of the forms while being, themselves, imperfect. These metaphysical ruminations concern the body in the sense that, while not a priority for Plato, the body is still a part of his works. From the walk outside the city one finds in the *Phaedrus*, to the comments on youth and fitness in *Theaetetus*, to Eryximacus's speech in *The Symposium*, Plato's writings are never far from grappling with the body. Thus, a binary relationship between body and mind emerges from Plato's work, establishing a pattern that will hold true for philosophy up until the late 19th century. While the body is not always denigrated as that which hinders the mind, it is, at least until Nietzsche, a secondary concern if it is a concern at all.

For René Descartes, the body is not important enough a topic to even consider. In his *Meditations on First Philosophy*, Descartes discusses the difficulties of grounding truth in an empirical foundation.[4] Yet this

2. Plato, *Republic*, bk. 6.

3. Plato, *Republic*, 509d

4. Descartes, *Meditations*, 59.

foundational account of knowledge discusses only the shortcomings of sense data in general; Descartes does not talk about the body as such. This neglect is seen even in the infamous account of other minds, where Descartes claims that the extent of one's knowledge through sensuous input only grants the subject the ability to refer to others as possible automata or self-moving machines.[5] Descartes' disinterest in the body is repeated in the work of the British Empiricists and also with Kant and the German Idealists that followed him. It is important to note that none of these thinkers are necessarily against the body outright. Rather, they are merely repeating the move made by Descartes and others, focusing on sensation *in general* and thinking *in general* and not considering the particularity of the body. This tendency towards generalization is repeated until the work of Friedrich Nietzsche.

One such example of how this generalizing tendency in philosophy unknowingly inherits the prejudice against the body can be found in Kant's ethics. For Kant, practical reason is the domain of the will.[6] It is not theoretical in the sense that the categorical imperative is not an epistemological activity, gathering data from the sensible manifold and subsuming it into the categories of the understanding. Instead, the will is the domain of ethical activity wherein one conforms one's actions to the form of the moral law.[7] To conform to the moral law is to do what is right independently of that towards which one is inclined. Indeed, inclination tends to operate in Kant's corpus as an analogue to the unregulated or disordered desire one finds in Plato's tripartite structure of the soul in *The Republic*. To be fair, inclination and desire are not explicitly linked to the body in Kant's practical philosophy—it is far too disembodied to make mention of that—but both concepts are not devoid of the philosophic inheritance that equates desire with the body. What results is an ethics that attempts to disentangle itself from the messiness of embodied experience, inclination, and pleasure in order to fully embrace the purity of duty-bound action.[8] At best, Kant's ethics exemplify the manner in which 18th and 19th century philosophy saw the body fade into the background and fail to become the interest of philosophical study. At worst, Kant's ethics echo the unthinking acceptance of traditional prejudices against the body that philosophers attempted to

5. Ibid., 63.
6. Kant, *Groundwork*, 49.
7. Ibid., 72.
8. Ibid., 52

escape. Such an evasion of the body and its entanglement with metaphysical prejudices is precisely where Nietzsche's work on the body picks up.

For Friedrich Nietzsche, the treatment of the body in the Western philosophic tradition is illustrative of the need for a transvaluation of all values. The body is the site of pleasure and finitude, two concepts Nietzsche identifies as despised by Western thought. To praise the pleasure, revelry, desire, passion, temporality, and passivity is, for Nietzsche, to worship at the feet of Dionysus. The Dionysian impulse is contrasted with the Apollonian impulse towards order, morality, reason, and activity.[9] Thus, according to Nietzsche's diagnosis of Western metaphysics, the obsession with purity, reason, and order has resulted in an Apollonian sickness.[10] The values of traditional Western thought must be overcome in order to escape the nihilism that lurks within Apollonian thought after the death of God. Nietzsche saw that this creeping nihilism exists in the hollowing out of authority and moral order through the continued lack of belief in transcendent Gods or principles or truth. It is not that Western civilization has thrown off the mantle of authority or transcendent truth; rather, it is that whatever claims to be authoritative or transcendent is arbitrarily constructed and therefore, hollow.[11]

Nietzsche's attempt to overcome this sickening nihilism was through the transvaluation of all values, wherein the Apollonian values of reason and order were overturned through *affirming life* in all of its messiness.[12] However, the affirmation of life is not synonymous with discarding one set of values and embracing a forgotten set of different values. Such an approach would be a repetition of the Christian Church's embrace of ascetic ideals. For Nietzsche, the ascetic eliminates passion by any means necessary. Yet, as Nietzsche points out, to eliminate the passions in order to do away with the difficulty they bring to those ideals of purity and reason held so dearly by Western thought is to engage in the very activity that brought about the problems in the first place. The problem, Nietzsche points out, is not with desire or with the body itself, it is with the hatred of the body and the moral methodology of asceticism. As Nietzsche says in *Twilight of the Idols*:

9. See Nietzsche, *The Birth of Tragedy From the Spirit of Music,* and Deleuze, *Nietzsche and Philosophy,* for further commentary on the relation between the Apollonian and the Dionysian.

10. Nietzsche, *Twilight,* 166.

11. Ibid., 171.

12. Ibid., 174

> The Church combats the passions with excision in every sense of the word: its practice, its 'cure' is castration. It never asks: "How can one spiritualize, beautify, deify a desire?"—it has at all times laid the emphasis of its discipline on extirpation (of sensuality, of pride, of lust for power, of avarice, of revengefulness).—But to attack the passions at their roots means to attack life at its roots: the practice of the Church is hostile to life. . .[13]

Thus, Nietzsche sets up the Church and Western thought in general as complicit in the hatred of life (insofar as life is tantamount to desire, passion, and the body). These ascetic practices aim to castrate the very means by which life is affirmed all in the name of salvation. Such is the insane logic of nihilism.

Yet Nietzsche's approach to the body is in service of his larger metaphysical project of transvaluing the values of Western culture and Christianity. Nietzsche is not a thinker of the body per se, merely the first philosopher to take it semi-seriously since Aristotle.[14] The body is one descriptor among others for the constellation of values Nietzsche names Dionysian. It is not an actual theme for philosophical investigation. Thus, even though Nietzsche breaks with tradition and holds the body to be important, he does not treat it with any of the depth and passion that he gives to his other concepts such as the will to power, nihilism, the critique of Christianity, and the problems with Wagner.[15]

PHENOMENOLOGY AND THE PHILOSOPHY OF THE BODY

Despite Nietzsche's emphasis on the body's importance, Western philosophy did not take the body seriously as a theme for inquiry until the

---

13. Ibid., 172.

14. I realize that I haven't said much about Aristotle in spite of his status as an exception to the tradition of disembodied abstraction in Western philosophy. However, Aristotle's inheritors did not inherit his emphasis on the body's importance as seen in such works as De Anima. One might excuse his omission on grounds that Aristotle is speaking as a scientist when we addresses the importance of the body but that doesn't fly when one considers the centrality of the hylomorphic union in his understanding of human beings. Aristotle is the exception to the neglect of the body in the history of Western philosophy leading up to Nietzsche but it will not be until Husserl's phenomenological philosophy emerges that the body becomes a theme for philosophical investigation.

15. For more on these themes, see Heidegger's two volumes of lectures on Nietzsche.

twentieth century. Specifically, the body was not treated in a systematic and rigorously philosophic manner until Edmund Husserl's work on phenomenology and materiality in *Ideas II*.[16] Husserl's phenomenology was and remains a method of philosophical investigation that attempts to describe and account for the experience of things themselves. It is a method of inquiry that has produced some of the most interesting and innovative philosophical, psychological, and sociological developments of the past hundred plus years. Phenomenology attempts to access the way in which objects appear and are given to consciousness on their own terms. As such, phenomenology has, in its long history, investigated such phenomena as language, selfhood, perception, social interaction, the body, and even Being itself. Husserl's *Ideas II*, and specifically its investigations into the lived experience of the body, was essential for the most well-known and influential work on the philosophy of the body to date: Maurice Merleau-Ponty's *Phenomenology of Perception*.[17]

In the *Phenomenology of Perception*, Merleau-Ponty identifies six criteria that characterize the experience of embodiment. The body is understood as an absolute here, as spatio-temporal, as movement, as expression, as transcendence, and as inter-subjective. These criteria emerge from investigations into the way in which human beings experience themselves as being embodied. The experience of embodiment is what Merleau-Ponty refers to, along with Husserl, as the *lived body* that is contrasted with the objective body of mechanistic physiology and classical psychology.[18]

For Merleau-Ponty, our manner of being in the world can be understood in the following way: If perception comes from somewhere, then it exists within a particular context that envelops all experience. This context of experience is one of the senses meant by the world in which one lives. This lived world is the meaningful context for all embodied experience and has a consistency relatively independent of the particular stimuli that forbids treating being in the world as the sum of reflexes. In this sense, being in the world establishes the juncture of the psychical (thought) and the physiological (body).[19] Being in the world means, therefore, that the body

---

16. Husserl, *Ideas Pertaining to a Pure Phenomenology and a Phenomenological Philosophy: Second Book: Studies in the Phenomenology of Constitution*.

17. Merleau-Ponty, *Phenomenology of Perception*. Husserl's *Ideas II* was not available in print form until well after Merleau-Ponty had published his work.

18. Merleau-Ponty, *Perception*, 82.

19. Ibid.

is the vehicle of lived experience and having a body means being tied to a definite environment of milieu, merging with certain projects and being perpetually engaged with both this milieu and the projects that occur within it. I am conscious of my body through the world and my body is the unperceived term at the center of the world toward which every object turns its face. My body is therefore the pivot of my world.[20]

Merleau-Ponty attempts to overcome the perceived separation of psychical and physical—as demonstrated in mechanistic physiology and classical psychology—through examining the phenomenal body or the body as it is lived, as it is through being in the world. These two parts, the psychical and the physical, are not things in themselves but are both oriented towards the intentions of the subject. Human beings are not a psyche joined to an organism but a back-and-forth of existence that moves between the body as objective or acted upon and the body as lived or active.[21] Embodiment is therefore to be understood as the experience of the body through being in the world. As such, the particular characteristics that make up the experience of embodiment reveal that the body is experienced as an absolute here, as spatio-temporal, as movement, as expression, as transcendence, and as inter-subjective.

Embodiment, understood phenomenologically, is intentional, absolute, spatio-temporal, transcending, expressive, and inter-subjective. It is also unintelligible without seeing embodiment as organized, acquisitive behaviors that occur within a certain milieu and surrounded by objects and others whose sense engages with the body in the back-and-forth movement of existence. Yet, the phenomenological approach, however influential, is not the only approach to the body taken by contemporary Western philosophy. One can look to the deconstructive work of Jean-Luc Nancy and his pair of *Corpus* books or to the gender-based approach of Judith Butler and her influential work *Bodies that Matter*. Nancy attempts to begin an ontology of the body in *Corpus*, by focusing upon the ontological status of bodies being both singular and plural. Bodies are multiplicities, organs, bacteria, limbs all bound together into a kind of singular projection, the mask of which is the ego. He resists a Cartesian ghost in the machine so much so that he reads Descartes against himself and reappropriates 'soul' to mean the self's experience of itself as body, a kind of interior/exterior revolution that never resolves. However, in spite of Nancy's appropriation

20. Ibid., 84.
21. Ibid., 90.

of Christian themes to articulate this new ontology, Wesleyan philosophy and theology has remained largely ignorant of his work.

From a social/political position, Judith Butler, as well as a host of other feminist thinkers and queer theorists, problematizes the body as a social structure, a site of performativity and projection that, again, is irresolvable into a kind of mass or thing that affirms stasis. Again, however, with few exceptions, Wesleyan thought, perhaps repelled or wary due to the overtly leftist political positioning of many of these theorists, has not deeply engaged with feminism, let alone Judith Butler, until relatively recently; and such engagement has addressed at least initially the social/political, rather than the body-as-such.

Taking a more pragmatist and neuro-scientific approach, one can look at the work of George Lakoff and Mark Johnson in their exhaustive study *Philosophy in the Flesh*. Neuro-science has brought a welcome change to Anglo-American philosophy, in that it repositions the question of reason *into* the body, requiring analyses of reason's function and import to address the embodiment of it in and through bodies. Acknowledging the role of emotion in reason, for instance, emerges out of an embodied understanding of reason that refuses the 'tripartite' structure that lurks throughout Western philosophy since Plato.

All of these approaches—phenomenological, pragmatist, feminist, and deconstructive—treat the body not only as an interesting area worthy of investigation but as an essential component in any and all philosophical approaches to matters of existential importance. Whether in the realms of epistemology, metaphysics, ethics, aesthetics, or politics, accounting for the importance and influence of the body is seen as a necessity for philosophical research.

THE BODY IN THEOLOGY

Turning now to Western theology, we find a similar pattern of neglect regarding the body.

As Sally McFague writes:

> Christians should, given their tradition, be inclined to find sense rather than nonsense in body language, not only because of the resurrection of the body, but also because of the body and blood of Christ in the bread and wine of the Eucharist and the images of the church as the body of Christ. Christianity is a surprisingly

"bodily" tradition. Nonetheless, there is a difference between these uses of body and the world seen as God's body: the latter is not limited to Christians or to human beings and it suggests, as the others do not, that embodiment in some fashion be extended to God. It is possible to speculate that if Christianity had begun in a time less dualistic and antiphysical than was first century Mediterranean culture, it might, given the more holistic anthropology and theology of its Hebraic roots, have been willing to extend its body metaphors to God.[22]

Likewise, if perhaps more ironically, some branches of Christianity have understood faith to be a mental assent to certain propositional statements, a mind-oriented decision that involves ideas and beliefs. Even in the Holiness movements of the nineteenth and twentieth centuries, which emphasize the emotional as well as the rational, the seat of the emotions is still the mind. In spite of the body of Jesus Christ, we have managed oftentimes to advocate for disembodied faith centered upon the soul.

We have traced out the history of the body from a philosophical-historical perspective; to do so from the theological side would be a book in itself. However, some trends that trace their way through the history of Christianity are worthy of note. The Church in its teachings over the course of centuries has continued to, tacitly or overtly, support a rendering of soul from body, and a subsequent devaluing, even depersonalizing, of the body. Early Church fathers understood God becoming flesh as an act of humiliation, undergone solely for a people lost to sin and death (Athanasius). Movements that were later condemned as heretical argued for an utter mortification of the material in favor of the spiritual: Nestorius, for example, simply could not allow for God to be body and die, and thus constructed an argument for 'two natures' that kept the divinity and humanity of Christ strictly separate—going so far as to claim, "Mary did not give birth to God, my friends. For what is born of the flesh is flesh, and what is born of the Spirit is spirit . . . "[23] Docetisim rejected the humanity of Christ altogether, claiming Jesus was spirit who only seemed human. While these teachings were later condemned, the fact that they resonated and had passionate followers in the early years of Christianity testify to the tension between materiality and spirituality with which the Church wrestled.

22. McFague, "The World as God's Body," 672.

23. Nestorius, Sermon 1, quoted in Cyril of Alexandria, *Five Tomes Against Nestorius*, li–lii.

In the Middle Ages, Thomas Aquinas borrowed heavily from Aristotle and framed the relationship between soul and body as that of form and matter, with the soul being the 'form' of the body. The soul is the non-material, active element of the body, and as such is separate from it, potentially if not actually.[24] Once again, Western theology privileges the non-material over the material, understanding the material as the site of (potential) sin, whereas the non-material is the site of activity, and is the shaper, the "former," of the material.

Particularly in the last several centuries, the body in Western theology has been the site of sin and decay, of mortification in all its forms, rather than a site of salvation. (Even a cursory examination of the evangelical obsession with sexual purity will demonstrate this.) In spite of the Apostle's Creed's claim to belief in the resurrection of the body, lay Christians have generally believed in the ascension of the soul to heaven immediately upon bodily death. John Wesley's approach to this topic is, as is normally the case with Wesley, both good and bad. Wesley's *Primitive Physick* argues for the care of the body, going so far as to recommend dietary rules, regular exercise, and 'cures' for various ailments. This demonstrates an ethic of care for physical suffering, to be sure. However, it is not an explicitly theological work in terms of laying out his understanding of the relation of body and "soul." Wesley adhered to the understanding of his day that the soul itself was the essential thing—that the human being is more than a body, and indeed this "more than" is what makes him, not a speck in the universe, but beloved of God. His argument takes on the flavor of Descartes far more than it reflects the reality of the body of Christ.

Thus, dualism and its discontents have penetrated current popular Christian theology. Bloggers and Internet theologians now work out the relation of soul to body with admirable, if slightly heretical, enthusiasm. Andrew Wommack, for instance, writes, "I've come to know I'm a spirit being who has a soul and lives in a body. But the real me is my spiritual person."[25] In fact, 'triunism' has really become the flavor of the day: a tripartite personhood consisting of spirit, soul, and body, as Wommack articulates above and many (many) others echo. While there is a simplicity and order to having a tripartite personhood (it echoes the Trinity; it uses Greek words), there is little to justify such an account from Scripture itself.

---

24. See *Summa Theologica*, "Treatise on Man," Question 76.

25. Wommack, "Spirit, Soul, and Body."

N.T. Wright felt compelled to address this in a variety of works, which he summarizes in the following (lengthy) passage:

> But I'm afraid I do regard the traditional Christian preaching about everyone having a "soul" which needs "saving" as now almost hopelessly misleading. In particular, I note that three terms commonly used interchangeably to refer to the non-material element within dualist anthropology—mind, soul and spirit (*nous, psyche* and *pneuma*), are emphatically not interchangeable . . . when Paul speaks of the conflict between the spirit and the flesh, the *pneuma* and the *sarx*, he certainly isn't referring to a conflict between the non-material element of the person and the material element. As has repeatedly been pointed out, most of the 'works of the flesh' in Galatians 5.19–21 could be practised by a disembodied spirit (jealousy, etc.). So, too, when Paul thinks of the *pneuma* at work he does not restrict its operation to non-material activities.[26]

Thus, we face a challenge as we propose to explore questions of embodiment from a "Wesleyan spirit." First and foremost, we may be reifying what we presume to problematize even in this title: for what is a "Wesleyan spirit," if not a disembodied element? Secondly, what contortions must we undergo to argue that our viewpoints, varied though they may be, reflect a necessarily *Wesleyan* spirit, given the obvious dualism that presents itself in Wesley's thought? In desperation, we fall back upon Wesley's own definition of a "Methodist":

> The distinguishing marks of a Methodist are not his opinions of any sort. His assenting to this or that scheme of religion, his embracing any particular set of notions, his espousing the judgment of one man or of another, are all quite wide of the point. Whosoever, therefore, imagines that a Methodist is a man of such or such an opinion, is grossly ignorant of the whole affair; he mistakes the truth totally . . . *But as to all opinions which do not strike at the root of Christianity, we think and let think.* So that whatsoever they are, whether right or wrong, they are no distinguishing marks of a Methodist.[27]

As such, our approach is a more diverse one than the title may suggest. Our contributors have focused on a wide array of topics pertaining to the body—gender, body modification, phenomenological experience, the

26. Wright, "Mind, Spirit, Soul and Body: All for One and One for All: Reflections on Paul's Anthropology in his Complex Contexts."

27. Wesley, *The Character of a Methodist.*

economics of the body—and utilize theories and thinkers far afield of traditional Wesleyan sources (whatever those may be). Nevertheless, these essays remain in the Wesleyan spirit for a number of reasons. First, while Wesley was indeed a man of his times, he nevertheless held to a rather broad view of the salvation of all creation, and thus, almost in spite of himself, his theology extends to the material as well as the spiritual. Second, Wesley himself addresses the body with care and with love (as demonstrates in his *Physick*). Third, the authors of these essays align themselves with the Wesleyan perspective—they are philosophers, pastors and theologians within the broader Wesleyan tradition who take seriously this heritage. While each essay does not address Wesley by name, the use of reason, experience and tradition as well as Scripture guides each one's project and informs their scope.

CHAPTER OUTLINES

The volume begins with Michael Lodahl's essay "Was There Room in Wesley's Anthropology for Any Body, Particularly that of the Lowly Jesus?," which explores the ways in which John Wesley's somewhat pronounced soul-body dualism precluded his recognition of the irreplaceable importance of the body for Christian faith and discipleship. Focusing on Wesley's two sermons entitled "What is Man?," Lodahl attempts to discern why the body is virtually missing from Wesley's anthropology. Then, granting Wesley's rather anemic acknowledgement of the bodily nature of human existence, and couching it within his cultural, intellectual and religious context, attention shifts to Wesley's Christology, a subject to which Lodahl has given attention in past writing. Given Wesley's often alleged dependence upon early Greek Christian theologians (such as Irenaeus and Gregory of Nazianzus), the reticence on Wesley's part regarding Jesus' body of flesh and blood, of bone and brain, sharing fully in the existence of "flesh," is disconcerting and requires serious remedial work to be done by Wesley's successors.

Eric Severson's chapter, "The Body Obsessed," investigates the role of the body in religious enthusiasm, with particular attention to the work of Jan Patočka, Jacques Derrida, Søren Kierkegaard and Emmanuel Levinas. The chapter reflects on the negative response to "religious enthusiasm" by John Wesley, and explores the philosophical and ethical dimensions of euphoric religious experience. Ultimately, Severson suggests to have a body is a fundamentally ethical situation, and to be bodily is to be already entangled with the neighbor who suffers.

We turn to questions of epistemology in the next section. Jonathan Heaps' contribution, "Reason's Apprehension: How Knowing Is and Is Not Like Getting a Grip," addresses the metaphor of grasping as significant for a kind of knowing. At first blush, prehension (grasping) prepares for manipulation and, *a fortiori*, the fulfillment of the interests of whoever lives at the end of the grasping arm. But a phenomenology of the origins of the grasp (as in Jean Piaget's observations of infants) reveals a wordless conversation between body and world, in which the hand yields to the object as much as objects yield to prehensile dexterity. Bernard Lonergan's phenomenology of intelligence elucidates how knowing is also a creative and dynamic response, and thus always also a submission to the way things are. Intellectual grasp, then, is a dynamic structure of conscious activities that creatively and responsively engages the world proportionate to it.

Matthew Bernico explores the "Body without Organs" in his essay: "Paranoid Perfection: The Body Without Organs and the Christian." Christianity, Bernico claims, is a religious discipline that puts bodies, both individual and social, in particular arrangements in order to produce a number of affects or desires within them. One fruitful trajectory in theorizing about desire in individual and social bodies is Gilles Deleuze and Felix Guattari's theory of the "a religious disciple." Through his exploration of Deleuze, Guattari, and John Wesley, Bernico suggests a jumping-off point for a Christian politics rooted in the redirection of Christian desire.

In the section *Church Bodies*, Joyce Konigsberg orients our attention toward our relationship to and with God *as embodied*. In "Divine/Human Relationships," she explores the God of Christianity as a relational God who desires connection and association with creation, especially humanity. God therefore utilizes theophanies, or divine appearances, to establish relationships and communicate with humans who are part spiritual in nature but also temporal, finite, and corporeal. These physical qualities of embodiment enable people to experience the world through their senses in addition to their intellect and imagination. Thus, given the capabilities and limitations of human nature, Konigsberg proposes that embodying God within imaginative, anthropomorphic language and other meaningful symbolic representations advances the understanding and significance of theophanies and facilitates divine-human relationships.

John Bechtold continues the exploration of the Church and embodiment with his analysis of Hegel and Eucharist. In "On Becoming What We Are," he explores the Eucharistic phrase, "This is the body of Christ- broken for you," from a Hegelian perspective. Hegel offers an important means by which to describe the embodiment of grace that takes place in sacramental practice. The grace of which Eucharist is a means, is already present in the body of the participant. Particularly within a Wesleyan context, this extant grace is descriptively called prevenient insofar as it is always already present.

Embodiment is not limited to Wesleyanism, of course, nor to the Church alone. In the section *Altered Bodies*, essayists explore the ways in which we modify our bodies for good or ill, and the manner in which we take up space. Brannon Hancock's "Fracturing: the Eucharist, Body Modification, and the Aesthetics of Brokenness" examines the aesthetics of brokenness in relation to Christian Eucharistic practice and the secular rituals of body modification subculture. In the Eucharist, the Body of Christ is taken, blessed, broken (fractured), and given for the life of the world. Yet outside the *ecclesia* exists a "community" of sorts that similarly esteems the body broken. Participants in the "body modification" subculture maintain a countercultural aesthetic which inverts and subverts traditional notions of beauty, celebrating the beauty of bodies marked and manipulated by processes of intentional wounding and healing, processes characterized by pain and blood and which permanently transform the body. By focusing on *brokenness* as a common theme of both Christian Eucharistic practice and the rituals of the body modification subculture, Hancock examines the various ways in which the rituals of these two strikingly divergent communities bear resemblances but also significant differences.

Amanda DiMiele's essay, "A Phenomenology of Anorexia Nervosa" tackles the difficult topic of eating disorders and their relation to human embodiment and the Christian church. DiMiele notes that the medicalized body is an object, a machine that is the sum of its parts. Under this model, eating disorders lie in some dysfunction of the machine, typically understood to originate in the brain. The problem is that anorexia is not experienced as a dysfunction. It is experienced as the controlled pursuit of one's own positive ends—typically, the transformation of one's self or one's world. In other words, the experience of anorexia more closely resembles a practical ethic. Medical science simply does not have the conceptual resources to account for anorexia understood this way. For that account,

DiMiele's paper turns to the phenomenology of the body found in the early work of Maurice Merleau-Ponty before offering a corrective for theologically dubious accounts of human embodiment found in popular Evangelical culture and the Church in general.

In "Listening to the Silence Surrounding Non-Conventional Bodies," Teri Merrick encourages us to listen to those marginalized by our categorizations, particularly those who are intersex or transgender. She highlights two significant and recurring themes about bodies and identity. First, intersexed children, at least initially, do not experience their bodies as ill-fitting garbs or dysfunctional possessions in need of fixing. Rather, their bodies are simply who they are. This supports the claim of some phenomenologists and theologians that our most primordial sense of self is that we are bodies, not that we inhabit or possess them. Second, throughout these narratives are repeated appeals to 'autonomy.' This is significant because appeals to autonomy, like appeals to other prototypical Enlightenment notions, have fallen into disrepute as masking appeals to the modernist construction of a self-interested, self-reliant, and essentially private ego. She shows that 'autonomy' as used here cannot be so construed and thus has a legitimate place in our ethico-religious discourse.

We close with Craig Keen's essay, "The Mutilated Body at (Intercessory) Prayer." Although it is certainly true that Western intellectual history has prioritized the non-corporeal over the corporeal, its regard for the corporeal has itself prioritized not the bodies that we meet on the street, in the field, and at table, but an abstraction, a fantasy body, characterized by integrity, wholeness, health, well being, authenticity, and totality. However, strikingly large numbers of afflicted human beings never get over their lacerations, but live and die in agony, unfixed. Indeed, it could be argued that we all live and we all die unfixed, that we are all cut and broken to the end, persons without integrity, authenticity, or well being. Rather than reifying wholeness and integrity as "Christian values," mutilated bodies (including that of Jesus) point us toward disintegration, an unforeclosable glory, peace, and freedom without satiety.

All of these essays aim to examine the ways in which embodiment, rather than being a secondary area of philosophical and theological investigation, is at the center of Christian reflection and practice. This is not to say that the authors and editors of this volume lay claim to any revolutionary thought. As the essays in the volume attest, Wesleyans are not the first to tackle the relation between Christianity and the body. Instead, our hope is that this volume contributes a different perspective to the larger conversation on religious practice and embodiment albeit from within that constellation of voices who speak with a Wesleyan spirit.

BIBLIOGRAPHY

Aquinas, Thomas. *Summa Theologica*. Edited by Anton C. Pegis. Cambridge: Hackett, 1997.

Butler, Judith. *Bodies That Matter: On the Discursive Limits of "Sex."* Boston: Routledge, 1993.

Cyril of Alexandria. *Five Tomes Against Nestorius*. Oxford: James Parker, 1881.

Deleuze, Gilles. *Nietzsche and Philosophy*. Trans. Hugh Tomlinson. New York: Columbia University Press, 1983.

Descartes, Rene. *Meditations Concerning First Philosophy*. Translated by Donald A. Cress. Cambridge: Hackett, 1999.

Heidegger, Martin. *Nietzsche: Vols. 1 & 2*. Translated by David Farrell Krell. New York: HarperOne, 1991.

Husserl, Edmund. *Ideas Pertaining to a Pure Phenomenology and a Phenomenological Philosophy: Second Book: Studies in the Phenomenology of Constitution*. Translated by Ted E. Kline and William E. Pohl. Boston: Kluwer Academic Publishers, 1989.

Kant, Immanuel. "Groundwork to the Metaphysics of Morals." In *Immanuel Kant: Practical Philosophy*, translated by Mary J. Gregor. Cambridge: Cambridge University Press, 1996.

Lakoff, George, and Mark Johnson. *Philosophy in the Flesh: The Embodied Mind and its Challenge to Western Thought*. New York: Basic, 1999.

McFague, Sallie. "The World as the Body of God." *The Christian Century* 115.20 (1998).

Merleau-Ponty, Maurice. *Phenomenology of Perception*. Translated by Donald Landes. Boston: Routledge, 2012.

Nancy, Jean-Luc. *Corpus*. Translated by Richard A. Rand. New York: Fordham University Press, 2008.

Nietzsche, Friedrich. *The Anti-Christ, Ecce Homo, Twilight of the Idols, and Other Writings*. Translated by Judith Norman. Edited by Aaron Ridley and Judith Norman. Cambridge: Cambridge University Press, 2005.

———. *The Birth of Tragedy and Other Writings*. Translated by Ronald Speirs. Edited by Raymond Geuss and Ronald Speirs. Cambridge: Cambridge University Press, 1999.

Wesley, John. *The Character of a Methodist*. http://www.umcmission.org/Find-Resources/John-Wesley-Sermons/The-Wesleys-and-Their-Times/The-Character-of-a-Methodist.

Wommack, Andrew. "Spirit, Soul, and Body." http://www.awmi.net/extra/article/spirit_soul.

Wright, N. T. "Mind, Spirit, Soul and Body: All for One and One for All Reflections on Paul's Anthropology in his Complex Contexts." http://ntwrightpage.com/Wright_SCP_MindSpiritSoulBody.htm.

John Wesley and the Body

CHAPTER 1

Was There Room in Wesley's Anthropology for *Any*body, Particularly that of the Lowly Jesus?

Michael Lodahl

JOHN WESLEY, AT EIGHTY-FOUR years of age, wrote a meditation on the question poignantly raised in the eighth Psalm, "What is man?" What is *adam,* the human being? What does it mean to be human? Wesley hews closely to the Psalmist's sense for the smallness of the human beneath the daunting expanse of the night sky. To his credit, he readily implements what he was learning about the universe from late eighteenth century natural philosophy. For instance, he gestures toward "those amazing bodies, the comets,"[1] but then tries to venture beyond those bodies to ask "what is even the orbit of a comet . . . [compared] to the space which is occupied by the fixed stars, which are at so immense a distance from the earth that they appear when they are viewed through the largest telescope just as they do to the naked eye?"[2] Today he undoubtedly would be equally amazed, indeed perhaps dumbfounded, to learn that some of those "fixed stars" he was peering at were actually entire galaxies with billions of stars—countless bodies, truly "amazing bodies," in virtually infinite worlds.

1. Wesley, Sermon 103, "What is Man?," 457.
2. Ibid.

"But what is the human being [in comparison] to this?"[3] Wesley was not given, especially, to citing Saint Augustine, but does so here; drawing from the opening paragraph of *Confessions*, the human is *aliqua portio creaturae tuae*—"some portion of Your creation." But, Wesley immediately adds, *quantula portio!*—"how amazingly small a portion!"[4] Again, we could suggest that, were he living today in the light of literally countless stars at utterly unimaginable distances from our eyes, his sense of wonder would be grandly and legitimately magnified.

But having begun to acknowledge human insignificance in this vast universe, Wesley balks. How, he asks, "may we . . . cure this fear" of our nothingness? It feels as though his reassuring reply arrives far too readily: "First, by considering what David [in Psalm 8] does not appear to have taken at all into his account, namely, that the body is not the man; that man is not only a house of clay, but an immortal spirit; a spirit made in the image of God, an incorruptible picture of the God of glory; a spirit that is of infinitely more value than the whole earth."[5] How odd, really, of David not to have taken all that into account.

Wesley, then, avoids the existentially crushing weight of even his perceived universe by denying that the body belongs essentially to human being. We humans, Wesley stipulates, are of an altogether different order than this strange, vast and overwhelming universe that threatens to engulf us. Indeed, not only is the human essentially "a spirit" but *a spirit that is of infinitely more value than the whole earth*. Wesley has moved terribly quickly from human insignificance (of body) to aggrandizement (of spirit). This dismissal of the body bodes poorly for a book that has posed the question, "In what way does John Wesley appropriate or challenge the Western tradition on these matters [of body and soul]?" Of course, it would be all too easy to pile on Wesley for his undeniably strong dualism of body and spirit—in which, no surprise, the spirit comes out on top (and comes out at death). It would be easy, even tempting, to revile him for his dogged refusal to heed the psalmist's testimony regarding the material human being's place in a material world—and that he opted instead to appeal to an ethereal spirit, this "immortal part"[6] that "David does not appear to have taken at all into his account" of the human. It would be easy, but not especially helpful. Wesley in this matter was certainly a man of his time.

3. Ibid.

4. Ibid., 459.

5. Ibid., 460.

6. Ibid., 60.

His second reassuring response in the face of the universe's immensity is stronger. He reminds us that God, as testified to in Holy Writ, has created human beings (and everything else). This Creator *is* "God, and not man: therefore my compassions fail not."[7] Our smallness is no hindrance to divine compassion.

Yet the vastness of the universe, even of Wesley's far smaller universe, beckons dangerously again, sucking at his mind like the gravitational pull of a black hole. He muses, "'Nay,' says the philosopher, 'if God so loved the world, did he not love a thousand other worlds as well as he did this?' It is now allowed that there are thousands, if not millions of worlds, besides this in which we live."[8] What is different today? Only that now we confidently can say the number is not millions, but billions, and very likely trillions and trillions of such worlds, even perhaps as ours.

Wesley, in his time, is not even ambivalent about this. "I answer, Suppose there were millions of worlds, yet God may see, in the abyss of his infinite wisdom, reasons that do not appear to us why he saw good to show this mercy to ours"—the mercy, presumably, of reasonably intelligent life— "in preference to thousands or millions of other worlds."[9] It is worth noting that, at this point, Wesley is willing to consider the scientific evidence available to him. If the notion of "the plurality of [habitable] worlds . . . were allowed by all the philosophers of Europe," he writes, "still I could not allow it without stronger proof than any I have met with yet."[10] But at least he was willing to consider stronger proof were it offered. He even delves into the arguments of seventeenth century astronomer and natural philosopher Christian Huygens (1629–1695), who, Wesley points out, had changed his mind about the likelihood of life on the moon after determining during a solar eclipse that the moon must have no atmosphere. And "neither have we any proof that the other planets [of our own solar system, of course] are [inhabited]," Wesley adds. We can add further that, while we still have no *proof* that other planets host life, I for one would wager that the odds are extremely high. But the salient point here is that Wesley, as we generally have come to know and to appreciate, was willing to allow the evidence to lead in an argument.

Wesley returned to the question "What is Man?" in a second homiletic essay in 1789. (He was eighty-six years old.) Perhaps we might take a

7. Ibid.
8. Ibid., 461.
9. Ibid.
10. Ibid., 461–62.

moment to appreciate the rather existentialist spin he places on the question in his opening line; this is no abstract philosophical query. "Nay, what am *I*? With God's assistance I would consider myself."[11] This time the question is not entertained in terms of the human place in a vastly spacious space; instead, the quest is pursued in terms of a carefully crafted analysis of the composition of the human being. Drawing upon the classic idea of the four cosmic elements of earth, air, fire and water, and mediating that idea through what would have been "the best current physiology available to Wesley" at the time,[12] he explores and appreciates the intricacies of the body—but only for four paragraphs. He hastens onward, in his words, to "find something in me of a quite different nature, nothing akin to any of these [elements]. I find something in me that *thinks*"[13]—*judges, reasons, reflects*—and he stipulates that this something is not and cannot be reduced to a function of the body. Not surprisingly, he identifies it as "the soul."[14] We might note, however—even if only in passing—that in the first sermon we examined, Wesley identified this "immortal part" as "spirit."

This time, it is "soul"—"But what *is* my 'soul'?" he asks. "It is an important question, and not easy to be resolved."[15] He quickly rejects the notion that the soul is simply a function of the body or reducible to physical processes. "But what am *I*? Unquestionably I am something distinct from my body. It seems evident that my body is not necessarily included therein [my 'I']. For when my body dies *I* shall not die; *I* shall exist as really as I did before."[16] This does appear to be a sizable leap in logic and well beyond, too, what experience could deliver. Perhaps it is noteworthy that Wesley does resort to the humbler claim, *it seems evident* that my body is not necessarily included in my sense of identity.

His explorations on this matter—or, more precisely, on this 'soul'!—need not detain us here. As far as I am concerned, he was dead wrong about this—this thorough (and understandable) captivity to a dualism in which the *I* who speaks is a soul lodged in a body—indeed, "my soul," which of course raises the further question regarding what it is that claims possession in the phrase "my soul." But even if Wesley was wrong, as I who am a convinced emergentist believe him to have been, I again desire to press the

11. Wesley, Sermon 116, "What is Man?," 20.
12. Ibid., 21.
13. Ibid., 22.
14. Ibid.
15. Ibid.
16. Ibid., 23.

point that he drew upon the cosmology, physiology, and anatomy that was generally available to him at the time. We know this. And we get to do the same thing—and we ought to. Unlike Wesley, we interpret ourselves to be living in a fourteen billion year old universe on a five billion year old planet, in a galaxy of unimaginable proportions that is but one of billions and billions of galaxies. We are stardust. We are the products of millions of years' worth of evolving life on earth. On this reading of things, "I" am a body, and whatever the language of "soul" or even a "spirit" might entail, I assume it to be an emergent property or function of the human brain, which is to say, of the body.

If, in the words of Wesley's earlier sermon, "the body is not the man," or in the words of the latter, "my body is not necessarily included [in my sense of *I*]," then it is not terribly surprising that his anthropological dualism would have Christological fallout. I am certain that it did. If the body is finally of negligible worth for us, how much less value does it possess for the Son of God? Perhaps a few examples will suffice. In his comments on Jesus's escape from his fellow Nazarenes in the hometown synagogue (Luke 4:30), Wesley suggested that Jesus eluded them "perhaps invisibly;"[17] when commenting on a comparable story in John (8:59), he mused, "Probably by becoming invisible."[18] It is striking that Wesley so quickly appealed to a disappearing act that seems strongly to imply that he had no issue with the notion that Jesus's human body could become invisible at will. In other words, this is not a body as we know it. Whatever we might speculate regarding the sudden appearances and disappearances of the resurrected Jesus in the gospels of Luke and John, surely we ought to exercise extreme caution, and even skepticism, regarding such possibilities for Jesus "during the days of his flesh" (Heb. 5:7).

Likewise, in commenting upon Calvary, Wesley cavalierly suggested that Jesus "could have continued alive, even in the greatest tortures, as long as He pleased, or have retired from the body whenever He had thought fit," that in fact he showed the extent of his love "inasmuch as He did not use His power to quit His body as soon as it was fastened to the cross, leaving only an insensible corpse to the cruelty of His murderers; but continued

---

17. Wesley, *Explanatory Notes Upon the New Testament*, 217, note on v. 30. To his credit, he then adds, "or perhaps they were overawed; so that, though they saw, they could not touch him."

18. Ibid., 342, note on v. 59.

His abode in it, with a steady resolution, as long as it was proper."[19] What Wesley here was attempting to describe is not the Word that *became flesh*; no, this begins to seem docetically as though the Word *slipped inside some skin for a while*, "as long as it was proper." This Jesus that Wesley describes is not a body—frail, vulnerable, passive, passioned, ruptured, broken or bleeding. This is the Logos in his "abode," and of course a temporary abode at that.[20]

Wesley's reticence regarding Jesus's body of flesh and blood, of bone and brain, sharing fully in the existence of "flesh," is disconcerting and even disappointing. In my view, the evidence is strong that he is not of much particular help with the questions that contemporary philosophers within the Wesleyan tradition might want to engage regarding the significance of the body—unless those philosophers are themselves fairly deeply convinced body-mind dualists. We can be kind to him, gentle with him, by remembering that he was a body in a particular place and time, as are we, deeply situated in a particular culture of thought with its attendant ruling assumptions. It is safe to say that most of us live in a very different intellectual world than did he. We can and should take heart, as I mentioned earlier, that he appears to have been quite willing to learn, to rethink his assumptions and commitments, in the light of new evidence. I think of a line from Mildred Bangs Wynkoop's *Theology of Love*, one perhaps too often overlooked. There she writes of her own book, "Only in Wesley's openness to the depths of truth do we consider this [book] to be Wesleyan"[21]—as though initially to suggest that her thought was Wesleyan in form but not in content, in open and adventurous spirit but not in substance. Perhaps that is the best claim we, too, could make for being "Wesleyan."

---

19. Ibid., 134, note on v. 50.

20. For a treatment of other dramatic instances of Wesley's strong reservations about Jesus as a truly human body, see Hambrick and Lodahl, "Responsible Grace in Christology? John Wesley's Rendering of Jesus in the Epistle of Hebrews," 86–103. Of course, John Deschner got this ball rolling over fifty years ago in his doctoral dissertation, written under Karl Barth's tutelage, *Wesley's Christology: An Interpretation*.

21. Mildred Bangs Wynkoop, *A Theology of Love: The Dynamic of Wesleyanism*, 77. It could readily be argued that Wesley's actual, day-to-day ministry, including his popular book of relatively inexpensive home cures, *Primitive Physick*, should be appreciated as a kind of corrective to his anemic Christology *and* his radically dualistic anthropology (under the assumption that he himself often employed, that a person's actual living may be a vast improvement upon her or his theology). In this light, perhaps there is hope that Wesley could even now help at least a little to point a way forward for contemporary Wesleyan reflection upon bodies in this material creation.

BIBLIOGRAPHY

Deschner, John. *Wesley's Christology: An Interpretation.* Dallas: SMU Press, 1960, 1985.

Wesley, John. Sermon 103, "What is Man?" In *The Works of John Wesley*, vol. 3, Sermons III (71–114), edited by Albert C. Outler. Nashville: Abingdon, 1986.

Hambrick, Matthew, and Michael Lodahl. "Responsible Grace in Christology? John Wesley's Rendering of Jesus in the Epistle of Hebrews." *Wesleyan Theological Journal,* 43.1 (2008) 86–103.

Wyncoop, Mildred Bangs. *A Theology of Love: The Dynamic of Wesleyanism.* Beacon Hill of Kansas City, 1972.

CHAPTER 2

The Body Obsessed

Reflections on Religious Enthusiasm

Eric Severson

FOR THIRTY DOLLARS ON Amazon.com, I purchased a bullroarer patterned after the kind used by native peoples in Australia and South America. Utilizing the Doppler effect, long before it was given that name, ancient shamans and religious leaders discovered a surprising reaction to the swinging of the bullroarer. Eerie and otherworldly sounds hummed and buzzed from the whirling device. I use the device in my World Religions course to help students understand the effect of such experiences on ancient and indigenous people. The vibrations, some exceeding the range of human hearing, evoke a sense of "numinosity in ritual participants."[1] The bullroarer is one of many tools used by people today and across the ages to create what might be categorized as a "religious experience." Hallucinogenic herbs and drugs are utilized all around the world to achieve a similar effect, though I do not recommend these for classroom demonstration. Shamans, yesterday and today, might dance and chant for hours, opening a channel to the secret mysteries beyond the everyday and the ordinary.

Religion, if we define it from its Latin root *religare*, binds the people to something. In the religious enthusiasm of Shamanic practices, the acts

---

1. Esposito et al., *World Religions*, 47.

of the shaman bind people to the mysterious, the secretive, the beyond. Such experiences crack the sky open. The visions and revelations that occur during these events are not like the data gathered in the daytime appropriations of the senses. Everyday events of gathering, storing and consuming are the labors of possession and acquisition. Our five senses are well honed for these enterprises. Bodily experience, in this context, is dispossession, an encounter with that which cannot be appropriated and possessed. Religious enthusiasm can provide a release from the typical way of knowing, grasping and making familiar. And though such experiences are noteworthy for their apparent transcendence of bodily experience, they are nothing if not bodily. This chapter will investigate the role of the body in religious enthusiasm, with particular attention to the work of Jan Patočka, Jacques Derrida, Søren Kierkegaard and Emmanuel Levinas. I begin and end, however, with John Wesley, whose emphasis on holy love made this question particularly poignant in his life and ministry.

Western philosophy, as well as Christianity, has struggled to find a stable place for the category of religious enthusiasm. John Wesley provides an intriguing example of someone who labored in the tension between rejecting and embracing religious enthusiasm. He attempted to steer through tricky waters, between the two monumental idolatries that threaten Christianity—and perhaps philosophy itself. One rocky reef is the complete embrace of reason and the rational powers of the human mind. The other peril is the idolatry that might arise from complete submission to the passions, and the consequent abandonment of reason. On the one hand too much trust is placed in (what Wesley called) "common sense" and "outward duties."[2] On the other there are endless dangers that arise when emotion and enthusiasm replace the substance of the Christian life. In his sermon on religious enthusiasm, Wesley calls it a "many-headed monster."[3]

The creature Hydra is one of the mythological monsters from the ancient Greek imagination. Hydra appears in the labors of Heracles, as the second challenge in his long journey to prove his heroism and valor. With many heads and venom so poisonous that even its tracks and breath are lethal, the Hydra possesses the daunting capacity to re-grow its severed heads. When Heracles cuts off one of its many heads, two grow in its

2. Wesley, *Sermons on Several Occasions*, 329ff. The sermon, "The Nature of Enthusiasm" is also know as "Sermon 37" and appears in many collections. Because of the plethora of editions of this sermon the citations below will refer to paragraphs rather than pagination.

3. Ibid., paragraph 32.

place. This would presumably discourage even the hardiest of opponents. Wesley's concern sits within a long Western philosophical and theological tradition that has focused attention on an ancient, nearly universal human tendency toward religious fervor.

Wesley's metaphor for religious enthusiasm invited a deeper examination of the way bodily excitation relates to theology and philosophy. The role of enthusiasm, and the way religion relates to the ecstatic bodily experiences, is of principle concern to the philosopher Jan Patočka. He deals with the question quite directly in his *Heretical Essays in the Philosophy of History*. Wesley's treatment of this subject quickly turns pragmatic; his primary agenda was not to provide the philosophical and anthropological roots of enthusiasm, but to help Christians live and worship rightly. Still, Wesley provides an intriguing opening for those who would think philosophically about bodies and religious enthusiasm in his wake.

Wesley's work is positioned in the midst of a modern era marked by a scathing critique of religious expression that gave into to bodily enthusiasm. Well aware of the tide of anti-enthusiasm that is a trademark of the enlightenment, and under some accusations that his Methodist movement was guilty of these extremes, Wesley expressed stern agreement with many of the concerns of the Enlightenment. Wesley was conversant with this modern project, and sympathetic toward some of the rationalistic impulses of John Locke, David Hume and others. At the same time, we find in Wesley an urgency to emphasize the way love for God and neighbor can carry one away, outside of the stability of the rational self. His sermon on religious enthusiasm takes as its orienting text Paul's defense before Festus in Acts 26. Festus says to Paul, "You are beside yourself!" or in other translations, "Paul, you are out of your mind!"[4] Festus, in this passage, operates as a rational judge for Paul's testimony about the cross. Paul insists that the despite the appearance of enthusiasm, he is "perfectly sober." This is a theme that stretched back to the earliest pages of the book of Acts, in fact. The followers of Jesus are accused of intoxication despite their sobriety. To abolish religious enthusiasm, then, is to dispense with something absolutely central to Wesley's love-centered articulation of the Christian story.

Yet in the context of eighteenth century England, Wesley had to be careful to distinguish the way Christian love relates to the bodies of believers. "Enthusiasm," Wesley claims, is an "uncouth," "dark, ambiguous word."[5]

---

4. Acts 26:24 NRSV.

5. Wesley, "The Nature of Enthusiasm," paragraphs 7 and 34.

He outlines many ways in which the madness of many forms of enthusiasm cloud and obfuscate true faith. Ironically, most enthusiasts demonstrate an "awkward mixture of real Heathenism and imaginary Christianity."[6] The primary reasoning behind these expressions, for Wesley, appears to be an intentional or unintentional dishonesty about the relationship between human experiences and the revelation of God. Most enthusiasm, he argues, is a "religious madness arising from some falsely imagined influence or inspiration of God."[7] As he unpacks the experiences and manifestations of enthusiasm, Wesley makes it clear that the deepest problem with fanaticism is that is it ultimately self-referential. Even when it purports to be aimed Godward, the fanatic is ultimately wrapped up in either heathenism or self-worship.

Wesley calls religious enthusiasm a Hydra precisely because it will never suffice to attack the problem in its individual instances. He lists a number of ways that enthusiasm may appear in the world, but to strike down one form is only to find that another, perhaps multiples, appear in its place. Wesley names a number of forms of enthusiasm, but is chiefly worried by the emotional fervor that would lead someone to claim that they are basking in the love and forgiveness of God while their lives still bear evidence to the contrary. Another brand of enthusiasm, according to Wesley, is the evident when people seek the *ends* of spirituality without submitting themselves to the means—specifically the means of grace. For Wesley, the deepest dangers of religious fervor become evident when enthusiasm threatens to veer its revelers away from the moral and spiritual moorings in human responsibility to God and neighbor.[8] There are many heads to this monster. It sometimes talks smoothly with a Hyrda's forked tongue, sometimes is characterized by euphoric and ecstatic worship, sometimes parades as a Pelagianism that subordinates the need for grace to the manufacturing of an experience. The question of religious enthusiasm continues to divide Christians and philosophers alike.

Philosophy has across history found itself routinely pitted against the pursuit of religious experience, even as it has routinely made peace with religion. The pre-Socratic philosophers work in earnest to undermine the traditional and religious interpretations of natural phenomenon. The epic poetry of Homer showcases such ancient appeals to the gods to explain

6. Ibid., paragraph 17

7. Ibid., paragraph 12.

8. Ibid., paragraph 37.

the apparently capricious behavior of land, seas and skies.[9] Philosophy is traditionally said to begin in Milesia, with Thales, Anaximander and Anaximenes, all of whom are first of all *naturalists*, inquirers into nature.[10] While philosophy has historically left room for *theism*, the idea of God, and even attempted to prove God's existence, it is no overstatement to summarize the history of philosophy as generally skeptical about religious experience. Philosophy has been particularly hard on religious enthusiasm, which seems at times to abandon the love-of-wisdom that is philosophy's namesake. Enthusiasm settles for charms, magic and sorcery. It fails, for that matter, because it takes leave of the body in the wrong direction. I turn to Jan Patočka in part because he helps elucidate both the dangers of enthusiasm and the insufficiency of reason.

A Czech phenomenologist and student of both Husserl and Heidegger, Patočka delivered a series of essays under the heading: *Heretical Essays in the Philosophy of History*.[11] Patočka claims that in a pre-religious stage, which he calls the demonic or orgiastic, religious fervor displaces responsibility, debt and separation.[12] Though his assessment of ancient and indigenous religious practices may be too sweeping and generalized, he identifies some intriguing results of impassioned religious practices. Religious enthusiasm acts, in part, as a liberation from the bodily constraints of the mundane and the profane. Patočka outlines a distinction between the sacred and the profane according to the heaviness and weight of banal, bodily existence and the religious experiences that allow someone to escape the burdensome boundaries of the flesh. In the sacred, which he also calls "demonic" and "orgiastic," revelers are transported from the workday to the feast, from the ordinary to the exceptional, and especially from inescapability to liberation.[13] Patočka imagines this form of religion, ancient and modern, as filled with mystery, fear, awe and release. In such a state one is liberated from the mundane chains of bodily existence. In the rapturous state that results, we are responsible only to the spirits or gods.

Shamanic, indigenous and ancient worship is more diverse than Patočka acknowledges, but his aim is not to provide a comprehensive history of religious enthusiasm. Rather, Patočka sets out to identify how

---

9. Stumpf and Fieser, *Socrates to Sartre and Beyond: A History of Philosophy*, 4.

10. Blackson, *Ancient Greek Philosophy*, 13–14.

11. Patočka, *Heretical Essays in the Philosophy of History*, 189.

12. Ibid., 105.

13. Ibid., 102.

religious enthusiasm is domesticated by Platonic philosophy. He suspects that there are unforeseen, "repressed" aspects of this primal, orgiastic impulses, and that his repression acts in part as a dangerous temptation to exchange responsibility for a private and rapturous experience.[14] It is Plato who embodies, for Patočka, the transition toward a higher evolution of human religious understanding. Plato moves the western religious imagination away from "striving for private and public orgiastic moments, sexuality and cult" and toward the rational polis, structured after a rational metaphysics of the *logos*.[15] This pushes religion past its "decadent" reliance on the escape from history and requires that ideas and experiences be universally submitted to a metaphysical system.[16] Plato, it seems, insists that if we are to move away from our bodies we must take leave of them in a different direction. The enthusiast leaves behind the flesh and lives in pure, unbounded relation to the divine. Plato's Good, however elevated, maintains a rational and metaphysical relation to the material we observe around us.

For Plato, we should remember, our bodies provide the very first rung on the Platonic ladder. In the *Symposium* we find that the beauty of the body can lead either to a deeper love for wisdom or to a shallow enthusiasm for the flesh. The movement up Diotima's ladder may, like the enthusiasm of the fanatic, move away from the banality of flesh. Yet Platonic ascension moves toward reason and rationality, not away from it. The body, in both cases, is a casualty of higher priorities. For Plato, the priority is the soul. For the "orgiastic" worship of the ancients, the body gives way to an unmitigated experience of the divine.

Patočka suggests that Plato enacts a kind of conversion to a new way of thinking about religion in the West. This Platonic "conversion" makes possible a universal vision for "the Good itself," a shared journey of all humans toward the same eternal goal.[17] The resulting religiosity prizes articulation, consistency, morality and rationality. Platonism is no atheism, and may be exactly the opposite; this tradition prizes and elevates the singular, divine Good. For Patočka, metaphysics is the "science of the divine," proceeding

---

14. Patočka uses the language of psychology to describe the various ways that ancient religious practices recede but remain dormant and concealed in Platonism and Christianity. Ibid., 13.

15. Ibid., 65, 103.

16. Ibid., 118.

17. Ibid., 105.

like science "in its aspiration to a global understanding of the whole."[18] Yet Platonic metaphysics, and the metaphysical enterprise in general, carries with it an internal contradiction that leads to its unsettling and eventual demise. Patočka's assessment of the demise of metaphysics is less important here than his point about the repression of the orgiastic that he believes Platonism retains. When metaphysical systems demonstrate their inability to connect with the everyday existence they are supposed to guide, the human tendency toward decadence again rears its head. And this is what Patočka suspects is the fate of twentieth century Europe, which falls to decadence as it looses its grip on universal metaphysics.[19] Jacques Derrida points out that Patočka's "orgiastic mystery" is never defeated, never successfully banished; it forever undermines any claim to pure authenticity.[20] Platonism, as Patočka understands it, unsuccessfully keeps the secret of its shamanic genealogy. The secret must remain secretive because Platonism is an idealism, thriving on the pursuit of mastery, knowledge, illumination and even deification.

The solution, for Patočka, is found in Christianity. This does not mean that Christianity succeeds in eliminated the demonic, but rather that Christianity acknowledges the *secretum* and therefore contains its menace. The mystery of Christianity lies in the relation between the human soul and the infinite but *personal* God. Patočka finds in Christianity's God a common direction for humans to fix their gaze, despite the fact that God is never fully subject to human vision or understanding. He writes, "the soul is not a relation to an *object*, however elevated (such as the Platonic Good), but to a person who fixes it in his gaze while at the same time remaining beyond the reach of the gaze of that soul."[21] The Platonic can provide ethics, can sustain the responsibility that is threatened and overturned by the demonic. But Patočka suspects that Plato has overestimated his ascendency from the frenzied depths of the orgiastic.

18. Patočka, "Negative Platonism: Reflections concerning the Rise, the Scope, and the Demise of Metaphysics—and Whether Philosophy Can Survive It," 188.

19. I must again register some caution in the face of Patočka's bold claims about Europe and metaphysics, which are too broad to be testable. The force of Patočka's argument does not depend, however, on whether he successfully describes all religious scenarious and situations.

20 Derrida, *Gift of Death*, 20–21. Derrida points out that Patočka's insistence on the survival of the demonic situates him closer to Friedrich Nietzsche than to Martin Heidegger.

21. Patočka, *Heretical Essays*, 116; Derrida, *Gift of Death*, 25.

For the Christian, as Søren Kierkegaard has repeatedly demonstrated, the ethical is insufficient. Platonic responsibility, inasmuch as it is self-justifying and self-referential, is never enough.[22] For Kierkegaard this is articulated in terms of the recalcitrance of sin, the resilient and persistent sinful bodies upon which the legs of Plato's ladder is founded. Sinfulness is not remedied by *ignoring* the problem or repressing the sense of one's inadequacy.[23] Nor is the sickness-unto-death of sin remedied by the extraordinary achievements of morality and responsibility. Faith, for Kierkegaard (or at least the pseudonym Johannes de Climacus), is an event in which the self rests "transparently in the power that established it."[24] The salvation of the self requires the opening of the closed ego to that which it can never incorporate, possess, synthesize or integrate. The roads of possession, synthesis and integration deliver us, for Climacus, to the despair that leads to death. The encounter with God, for Kierkegaard, is an encounter of an entirely different sort than the everyday encounters in being. Sin's inevitability and inescapability is interrupted. And we should therefore not be surprised to see, in the interruption of bodily inevitability, that those who revel in this grace wave hankies and run isles with euphoria that resembles shamanism.

Nonetheless, we are left with the question: do the bullroarer and the hankie represent two instances of the same phenomenon? This is perhaps the discussion that often goes missing when readers turn to Kierkegaard's *Fear and Trembling*. The text appears to narrate what Patočka would call an orgiastic sacrifice, and Abraham is praised for his faithful willingness to participate in an event that civilized contemporaries justifiable deem barbaric. But what Kierkegaard's Johannes de Silentio is out to demonstrate, in part, is that which differentiates Abraham from the demonic/enthusiastic/orgiastic. And this is the theological and philosophical problem at stake in our discussions today about religious enthusiasm. Silentio repeatedly reminds his reader that Abraham could pass very easily for a madman. He, like Paul, appears to be quite "beside himself." So how can we tell Jephthah from Abraham?

All of this is on Derrida's mind when he opens Patočka's essays on the history of philosophy, and begins to reexamine the way Christianity retains and preserves and contains the demonic, the orgiastic. The *gift* that is Christian salvation is not an accomplishment of the soul, as in Platonism,

22. See, especially, Kierkegaard, *Fear and Trembling*.

23. See, especially, Kierkegaard, *Sickness Unto Death*.

24. Kierkegaard, *Sickness Unto Death*, 14.

but that which is received from beyond understanding, as mystery. The wisdom of philosophy must be interrupted by that which it hoped had died or been forgotten. Platonism has failed to vanquish religious enthusiasm, in part, because it retains the structure of the orgiastic in its DNA. By this reading, Christian faith is in part an instance of enthusiasm making its reappearance. But Patočka may leave too thin a margin between the demonic and the holy, as though Christianity's *mysterium tremendum* and the orgiastic are distant cousins.

For Patočka, Platonism attempts to reorder the movement of possession. Rather than being possessed by the numinous other, as in orgiastic and cultic practice, the Platonic imagination audaciously attempts to possess and understand the divine. Patočka's Christianity leaves the believer without any possible possession of salvation. To be saved is not to draw from any resources native to the body, to the self. The salvation that can be hoped for must arise as gift, arising from a mystery not derived from any other truth or facet of fleshly existence. Socrates, on the other hand, declared that we "receive nothing of the other but what is in me, as though from all eternity I was in possession of what comes to me from the outside."[25] But this is, for Kierkegaard, the recipe for despair unto death; the solution to sin cannot be found in that which is already the possession of the self. And so one must first be dispossessed and then possessed by God.

Yet what does enthusiasm look like on the other side of this conversion? There are many components of the DNA of Patočka's orgiastic that appear in contemporary religious expression. Emmanuel Levinas claims that Judaism has "decharmed the world," identifying the idolatry of enthusiasm and its manner of elevating the human toward the divine.[26] Yet for Levinas, the new situation is not one in which the relation to the other person has become utterly secularized. Religious enthusiasm is instead a sober dispossession of self-interest. But it is not enough to be simply divested of self-interest, which is one of the purported virtues of modern philosophy.[27] For Levinas, one is utterly dispossessed. Levinas did not engage the work of Patočka on this theme, and in fact would prefer to state that to be possessed by the other, by God, is not to arrive at the pinnacle of the evolution

---

25. Levinas, *Totality and Infinity*, 43.

26. Levinas, "Religion for Adults," 14.

27. For a fascinating study of the role of disinterest in philosophy since Descartes, see Sean Gaston's *Derrida and Disinterest*.

of religion but to discover that religious enthusiasm has more than one heritage. The way Levinas proposes escape is an entirely new path.[28]

Levinas, unlike Patočka, suggests that the enthusiasm of love is not another stage in human religious development but the critique of religion in its many-headed monstrosities. Religion is the elevation, striving, possessing and achieving of the ego. As with Hydra, to scold one religious expression because it leaves revelers too sweaty or worked up is to miss the point and only engender more subtle and insidious forms of "human elevation."[29] To be soberly *possessed* by the other is to be responsible for the suffering of the other without any recourse to chain such responsibility back to a system of ethics. The sober bodily possession is more like obsession: an event in which the needs of the other have categorically consumed the attention of the self.[30] Such an event relates to the body in another manner entirely, unlike the movements of the orgiastic or Platonic. For Levinas, one finds that to have a body is to owe it to the other, to the neighbor who suffers. To have flesh is to carry around that which is not mine, that which is borrowed from the other.

So we find our way back to Wesley, who knows that there is nothing truly in common between the enthusiasm that leads to chest-thumping and fiery persecution of others and the enthusiasm that leads to dying for one's neighbor. Perhaps Patočka is right, inasmuch as we are tempted by the soaring emotional highs of the orgiastic, the demonic. Wesley would not hesitate to call these temptations the lure of the demonic. Wesley appears to have sensed that enthusiasm has multiple genres and origins. There is an enthusiasm that masquerades as love for God and neighbor, but it is fruit of an utterly different tree. Both carry the self outside the realm of reason, beyond what Johannes de Silentio calls "the ethical" or "the universal." Both possess the self from the inside out. Both demonic and holy enthusiasm are events in which the encounter is with the radically new, the other that is anything but Socrates' "already in me."

To reject religious enthusiasm is to seal off both genres, though probably unsuccessfully. The rejection of this opening to the infinite, to the radical other, is ultimately unsuccessful anyway—like Heracles severing

28. "Getting out of being on a new path." Levinas, *On Escape*, 73. Levinas' early and sustained critique of Heidegger focuses on the fact that Heidegger's path remains enthralled by myth and mythology.

29. Levinas, "Religion for Adults," 14.

30. For Levinas' reflections on "obsession," which he ties closely to the phenomenon of consciousness, see *Otherwise than Being or Beyond Essence*, 101.

another head from the Hydra. But the manifestations of religious enthusiasm, by Wesley's assessment, only appear to spring from the same source. Love that is truly without self-interest originates beyond any emotional uprising, beyond any Stoic *apatheia*, beyond any structured morality in the tradition of Plato. The sober enthusiasm advocated by Wesley will be marked by gratuitous hospitality, by an extravagant responsibility that precedes and interrupts both the euphoria of the demonic and the egocentrism of the ethical. Paul is indeed, as Faustus accused, beside himself.

To be for-the-other is to be *out of my mind*. It is because Abraham was "beside himself" that he recognized the voice of God as he gazed at the "kill me not" etched in Isaac's face. It is because Jepthah was *not* beside himself, but precisely within himself, that he missed the ram struggling in the thicket nearby. Holy enthusiasm is that which wrenches the ego into the possession of the other, of God, and in so doing divests the ego of its role as protagonist in the relation that unfolds. Faustus accused Paul of being "beside" himself.[31] The holy madness of responsibility carries me precisely beyond possession of my body, to the beside-myself, where stands the one who suffers, the stranger, the widow, the orphan, and the neighbor.

31. Acts 26:24 (NRSV).

BIBLIOGRAPHY

Blackson, Thomas. *Ancient Greek Philosophy.* West Sussex, UK: Wiley-Blackwell, 2011.

Derrida, Jacques. *The Gift of Death.* Chicago: University of Chicago Press, 1995.

Esposito, Fasching, et al. *World Religions Today.* New York: Oxford University Press, 2009.

Gaston, Sean. *Derrida and Disinterest.* New York: Continuum, 2005.

Kierkegaard, Søren. *Fear and Trembling.* Cambridge: Cambridge University Press, 2006.

Levinas, Emmanuel. *On Escape.* Stanford: Stanford University Press, 2003.

———. *Otherwise than Being or Beyond Essence.* Pittsburgh: Duquesne University Press, 1991.

———. "A Religion for Adults," *Difficult Freedom.* Baltimore: John Hopkins University Press, 1990.

———. *Totality and Infinity.* Pittsburgh: Duquesne University Press, 1961.

Patočka, Jan. *Heretical Essays in the Philosophy of History,* trans. Erazim V. Kohák. Chicago: Open Court, 1996.

———. "Negative Platonism: Reflections concerning the Rise, the Scope, and the Demise of Metaphysics—and Whether Philosophy Can Survive It." In *Jan Patočka: Philosophy and Selected Writings,* edited by Erazim Kohak. Chicago: University of Chicago Press, 1989.

Stumpf, Samuel Enoch, and James Fieser. *Socrates to Sartre and Beyond: A History of Philosophy.* Boston: McGraw-Hill, 2008.

Embodied Epistemologies

CHAPTER 3

Reason's Apprehension

How Knowing Is and Is Not Like Getting a Grip

Jonathan Heaps

IF THERE IS SUCH a thing as "Christian philosophy" (let alone a distinctly "Wesleyan philosophy"), I take theological epistemology to be one of its central tasks. The Socratic tradition echoes the Delphic inscription to us: "Know thyself!"[1] The Bible's prophetic tradition exhorts us, "let us press on to know the LORD."[2] Jesus, undoubtedly speaking out of that same prophetic tradition, told his disciples, "If you know me, you will know my Father also."[3] The Wesleyan philosopher, carrying the weight of all three traditions, can little ignore the question, "Whether myself, God, or anything else, what am I doing when I am knowing?"[4] Nor can the Wesleyan philosopher set aside certain limit cases of knowledge (what we might call

---

1. See Plato, *Charmides*, 164D; *Protagoras*, 343B; *Phaedrus*, 229E; *Philebus*, 48C; *I Alcibiades*, 124A, 129A, 132C.

2. Hos 6:3 (NRSV).

3. John 14:7 (NRSV).

4. Bernard Lonergan lists this as the first of three philosophical questions. "Why is doing that knowing?" and "what do I know when I do it?" complete his list. The answer to the first question is a theory or model of cognitional activity, and the answers to the second and third are an epistemology and a metaphysics, respectively. See Lonergan, *Method in Theology*, 2nd ed. 25.

"religious knowledge") to simplify her effort to answer this question. To put the question another way: the divine may call us to knowledge, but do we really know what knowing is?

In much the same way that her inherited traditions (namely, the Socratic, the prophetic, and the Christian) will not allow a philosopher to *a priori* exclude the transcendent from epistemological considerations, that same inheritance (never mind the very topic of this volume) will not allow theological epistemology to neglect the philosophical import of our embodiment. If Plato's writings left any ambiguity about the role of bodies in philosophy, Aristotle swiftly corrected it in favor of the material. Any reader of the biblical prophets can attest to the embarrassingly embodied quality of their thought. And beyond all of this, of course, there is the radical affirmation of human embodiment made by God in the Incarnation, about which so much could be said that I hesitate even to begin. If a Christian philosophy calls for a theological epistemology, it calls just as much for an *embodied* theological epistemology.

And yet, the effort to think the epistemological import of our embodiment walks a thin ridge, beset on either side by dangers. On one side, the task faces a vertiginous slope of reductionism that dumps out onto the sterile lowlands of physicalism. On the other side, we stare into fjords of Cartesian dualism, glacially carved by nearly three centuries of modern thought. Can we cut a path between these alternatives and avoid treating our conscious, intelligent experiences as epiphenomenal, but also avoid making our conscious intelligence *so* unique that our bodies become a matter of philosophical indifference?

This essay will consider two approaches at establishing such a path by applying bodily analogies to describe kinds of conscious, intelligent experiences. The first is the theological epistemology Jürgen Moltmann's work invokes all but in passing. The second is Jean Piaget's study of perceptual, motor, and intellectual development. I will also attempt to show how one of those approaches can be extended, with the help of Bernard Lonergan's philosophy of understanding, beyond mere analogy and toward a fully theoretical model of human cognition. The adequacy of that model will be measured by its ability to account for *both* the continuity of cognition with bodily engagement with the world *and* the irreducibility of cognition to the same.

MOLTMANN'S ANALOGIES

In a number of his major works, theologian Jürgen Moltmann contrasts two modes of knowing, each of which he describes on a bodily analogy. The first mode of knowing is like perception: it is a receptive openness to intellectually "see" what is there and, presumably, not see what is not there. Knowing-as-seeing lets beings be.[5] The second mode of knowing is like grasping: it circumscribes and manipulates objects. For Moltmann, this is the regrettably dominant form of modern knowing. In knowing-as-grasping, the interests of the knower are imposed on the known and this imposition transforms the known into an unrecognizable artifact that now stands between the knower and *das Ding an sich*. Knowing-as-seeing is thus true knowing, but knowing-as-grasping is not really genuine knowing.

Moltmann's analogies rest on a more basic dichotomy between a principle of similarity and a principle of difference underlying both epistemology and ethics. In 1974's *The Crucified God*, Moltmann writes, "(Aristotle's) social principle 'like seeks after like,' corresponds on the epistemological level to the Platonic principle 'like is known only by like.'"[6] In 1997's *God for a Secular Society*, he reiterates, "The principle of correspondence in epistemology and the principle of homogeneity in sociology correspond precisely."[7] According to Moltmann, "the principle of correspondence does not lead to any increase in knowledge, but only to continually reiterated self-endorsement of what is already known."[8] Thus, the principle of similarity only generates anemnetic solipsism.

The principle of difference, by contrast, understands knowing as the direct encounter of other with other. This principle of difference generates genuine knowledge, genuine learning for Moltmann, and also genuine community in diversity. Immediate encounter with the other becomes the measure of knowing not just otherness in particular, but anything at all. In this regard, Moltmann initially acknowledges a mediating role for analogy. Encounter with the same can carry some element of the other across to the subject. By 1999's *God for a Secular Society*, however, Moltmann will have rescinded the role of analogy in his theological epistemology. "In

5. Regarding the disclosedness of beings as a condition of truth (*aletheia*) and phenomenological receptivity, see Heidegger, *Being and Time*, 256–73.

6. Moltmann, *Crucified God*, 26.

7. Moltmann, *God for a Secular Society*, 136.

8. Ibid., 139.

epistemology," he writes, "must we not start from the principle '*Other is only known by other*,' and in sociology from the principle '*The acceptance of others creates community in diversity*'?"[9] The principle of analogy is pushed towards the circumscriptions proper to strict similarity and the principle of difference is expanded to include some of the intermediating functions of analogy. Moltmann writes,

> We know by analogy when we ask about the *tertium comparationis*, the factor linking the two elements we are comparing. In the spheres of those that are different, the knower always perceives only what is similar—that which corresponds to him. Why? Because he perceives only that which finds a correspondence in his own inner life. The macrocosm without corresponds to the microcosm within.[10]

When the principle of similarity (or even the ostensibly mediating principle of analogy) predominates, we can experience what is "next" but not what is "new." The progressive expansion of knowledge by analogy systematically excludes novelty and difference.

The two analogies now situated within the general context of the dichotomy above, Moltmann may narrate the relationship between the two modes of knowing as a fall from the ancient and contemplative knowing-as-seeing to the modern and manipulative knowing-as-grasping.[11] He writes,

> Ever since Francis Bacon and René Descartes, to know has meant to dominate. I want to perceive nature outside myself in order to dominate it. I want to dominate it in order to acquire it for myself. I want to acquire it for myself in order to do what I want with my possession. That is *thinking with the rapacious hand*: I grasped that—I've mastered it—I've got it—I've seized the meaning—I have it. In the modern civilization to which we give the name 'scientific and technological,' reason is no longer *an organ of perception*; it is now an instrument of power (emphasis added).[12]

Moltmann makes this point even more explicitly in *The Trinity and The Kingdom of God:*

9. Ibid., 136.

10. Ibid., 137.

11. Moltmann, *Trinity and the Kingdom*, 9; *Secular Society*, 139.

12. Moltmann, *Secular Society*, 139.

Modern thinking has made reason operational. Reason recognizes only 'what reason herself brings forth according to her own concept.' It has become a productive organ—hardly a perceptive one any more. It builds its own world and in what it has produced it only recognizes itself again. In several European languages, understanding a thing means 'grasping' it. We grasp a thing when 'we've got it.' If we have grasped something, we take it into our possession. If we possess something we can do with it what we want.[13]

The manipulations effected by prehensile kinds of knowledge are not just a form of domination for Moltmann, but also render knowledge blind to anything besides the *products* of its manipulations, à la the principle of similarity. "Wherever we look, we see only the projections, the reflections and the traces of human beings."[14] As noted above, prehensile knowing produces constructions and these constructions stand in between the person and *das Ding an sich*.

Luckily, there remain for Moltmann the perceptive ways of knowing employed by the Greek philosophers and the Church Fathers. "Reason was then essentially an observing reason (*theorein*), a *thinking with the eyes which see what is there*."[15] It offers genuine knowledge through immediate encounter. He also notes that, in the Ancients' perceptual knowing, the operational dynamic is reversed: "according to the view held in antiquity, perception changes the perceiver, so that the perceiver corresponds to what he perceives."[16] It fills us with the *really real* and makes us (it is implied) more real ourselves. Thus, contemplative "seeing" offers immediacy and transformative communion with alterity, where scientific "grasping" can offer only manipulation and occlusive sameness. The epistemological implications of this alternative can be extended, with deeply troubling effect, into the field of mutual knowledge that, at least in part, constitutes our interpersonal relationships. It is bad enough to distort one's apprehension of the world through epistemological self-assertion, but one transgresses into ontological violence when another person is manipulated and misrepresented in one's zeal for knowledge and control. Once again, the immediacy and receptivity of knowing-as-seeing is to be preferred on epistemological, sociological, and ethical grounds.

13. Moltmann, *Trinity and the Kingdom*, 9.

14. Moltmann, *Secular Society*, 140.

15. Ibid., 139.

16. Ibid., 141.

EVALUATING MOLTMANN'S ANALOGIES

Moltmann's bodily analogies for knowing, then, are not only descriptions, but also constitute a dichotomy of opposed alternatives. If, however, these analogies prove questionable, then Moltmann's dichotomy and its implications must come into question as well. First, if genuine knowing is something like seeing, then one ought to ask whether seeing is in fact the immediate and passive receptivity Moltmann describes. Is seeing a matter of just looking at what is there to be seen? There are good reasons to believe that, in the most relevant respects, it is not. Though the spontaneous experience of healthy, adult perception seems direct, immediate, and predominantly accurate, the work of psychologist Jean Piaget has shown that this experience results from the emergence of active psychological interventions that regulate against the distortions inherent in the passivity of ocular perception. Indeed, seeing approaches something like objectivity precisely by ceasing to be purely and passively receptive. Second, we will extend a similar suspicion to Moltmann's characterization of grasping. Is grasping really an unidirectional imposition of power and control upon an object by a subject? Again, there are good reasons in Piaget's analysis of the emergence of prehensile dexterity in children to suggest that it is not. Thus, there are good reasons to doubt the implications Moltmann draws from his analogy with grasping.

Against the Pure Receptivity of Perception

In a 1947 summary of his studies of psychological development in children, *The Psychology of Intelligence*, Piaget provided two examples that reveal the distortions structurally inherent in visual perception. The first is called "Delboeuf's illusion." A subject is successively shown two circles, each with a 15mm radius, but one circle has a 13mm circle drawn inside of it. This second circle, with the smaller circle inside of it, will appear larger than the isolated circle. Furthermore, if one incrementally increases the diameter of the larger circles, leaving the interior circle the same, the illusion is diminished in inverse proportion to the increase, approaching zero at a diameter of approximately 36mm. If one continues to increase the "outer" circles' diameters, the illusion inverts itself, producing an under-estimation of the "inner" circle.[17] Piaget suggested that this instance is a particular case of a general process. He writes,

17. Piaget, *Psychology of Intelligence*, 67–68.

If the standard is over-estimated (or, in certain circumstances, the variable) it is simply because the element which is fixated longest (or most often, or most intensely, etc.), is by the this very fact magnified, as though the object or the region on which vision is concentrated occasioned an expansion of perceptual space. . . *Perceptual space then is not homogenous but is centralized from moment to moment,* and the area of centralization corresponds to a spatial expansion, while the periphery of this central zone is progressively contracted as one proceeds outward from the center, (emphasis added).[18]

Piaget referred to this distorting effect of perceptual centralization (which affects the tactile sense also) as "perceptual relativity." Seeing is always seeing from a particular spatial relation to the seen, and the focal selection required to bring the seen into clear view picks out a certain portion of the visual field as "centered." Though this centering brings that portion of perceptual space into clarity, it exaggerates contrasts perceived in the periphery of that perceptual space.[19]

This effect can be mitigated by multiplying (automatically, in the healthy adult) the aggregate of centerings pertaining to a particular instance of the seen. According to Piaget's studies, "several distinct centerings correct one another's effects." This co-ordination of different centerings or what Piaget called, "decentralization," functions as an actively intervening, regulating, and correcting factor, except in cases where the distances involved preclude it, as in the Delboeuf illusion.[20] In those cases, the distortion proper to the mere receptivity of vision is revealed. Moreover, even this regulated correction produces not strict objectivity, but a statistical aggregate from which our reliable perceptions emerge as a kind of mean.[21] In short, even when we are actively (and, in the healthy adult, automatically) mitigating the distorting effects of perceptual centralization, we are still not directly, immediately, or entirely objectively seeing what is there to be seen.[22] In Piagetian terms, visual perception suffers a limitation in "mobility" because of its inherent relativity, which is to say that changes in spatial location produce uncompensated changes in perception.

18. Piaget, *Intelligence*, 72.

19. Ibid., 74.

20. Ibid., 72.

21. Ibid., 77–78.

22. For more detail on the process by which perceptual regulation and coordination emerge in infant development, see Piaget, *Origins of Intelligence in Children*, 62–76.

These uncompensated changes also show up in temporally successive presentations and regularly distort perception. One instance of such distortions is "Weber's Law," which states, "the size of 'differential thresholds' (smallest perceptible differences) is proportional to that of the elements compared."[23] Piaget explains using the example of perceived weight,

> Absolute differences are not discerned since 1 gram may be perceived when added to 1 gram although not when it is added to 100 grams. On the other hand, when the elements differ markedly the contrasts are then accentuated, as is shown in the ordinary cases of relative centralization, and this reinforcement is again relative to the sizes of the values involved (thus a room seems warm or cold according as one comes form a place with a higher or lower temperature). Thus, whether we are concerned with illusory similarities (threshold of equity) or illusory differences (contrasts), perceptually they are all 'relative.'[24]

Not only, then, is visual perception subject to synchronic spatial distortions, but also diachronic distortions due to the interaction of successive perceptual presentations. Skiers may note this effect when they remove red or green tinted goggles on a sunny day and find their visual field tinted in a contrasting hue for a short period of time. Vision, then, also has limited "reversibility" due to its relativity, which is to say that successive changes in perceptual activity impinge on the contents of directly subsequent perceptual acts.[25]

In short, Piaget's psychological studies isolate and analyze paradigmatic examples of how our spontaneous experience of perception as direct,

23. Piaget, *Intelligence*, 74.

24. Ibid., 75.

25. Acts of knowing that fail to transcend the limitations of perceptual relativity will be marked with this same quality. Piaget argued that in the causal reasoning of his experimental subjects from ages four to seven, an analogous distortion is at play. He called it "intuitive thought" and he found it was largely modeled on already established perceptual schemata. In intuitive thought, hypotheses cannot be put forth, tested, and then retracted without affecting the plausibility of successive ideas. Even though a hypothesis has not been born out by successive experiences, its failure does not wipe the mental slate clean. Successive ideas are not allowed to conflict with the previous idea, even though the child may explicitly acknowledge the previous idea has failed. Thus, this is another instance of limited reversibility. Facility with logical "reversibility" has to develop and reach a stable equilibrium before it can be regularly employed in the reasoning of the child (around age eight or nine). Before that, causal reasoning is subject to the same relativity as perception (see Piaget, *Intelligence*, 129–39).

immediate, and predominantly accurate has its origins in a complex process of actively intervening regulations that mitigate the distortions produced by perceptual relativity. "Perceptual relativity," he writes, "is distorting relativity, in the sense in which conversational language says, 'everything is relative,' when denying the possibility of objectivity; the perceptual relation modifies the elements which it unites, and we now understand why." Moreover, "these distortions are reduced by equally partial decentralizations."[26] Moltmann's epistemological analogies, then, prove to be founded on a common sense mythology of perception that rigorous study of the structures of perceptual constancy must implode. This, of course, leaves dangling and unsupported those ostensibly laudable qualities of ancient, contemplative knowledge that Moltmann derived from this analogy. As H. L. Mencken noted, there is always a well-known solution to every human problem that is "neat, plausible, and wrong."[27]

Against the Purely Manipulative Grasp

Furthermore, Piaget's analysis of sensori-motor development suggests that grasping objects is not the naked act of self-assertion that Moltmann takes it to be. On Piaget's analysis, healthy human infants are born with a grasping reflex, but, in this (literally) nascent form, it is only effective on a limited range of objects. Most human fingers are a good fit, but so are hoop-earrings, unfortunately. At first, a baby will struggle to hold almost anything not conforming to this limited range. As dexterity improves, however, the skill for grasping will be "generalized" to a wider and wider array of objects. At once, the world of graspable objects will expand and the grasping skill will gain mobility within that world. Though we can observationally distinguish subject and object with Piaget, in the infant, self and world develop as undifferentiated coefficients.

For Piaget, the generalization of the grasping reflex proceeds by "adaptation," a dialectical process of what he calls "assimilation" and "accommodation."[28] On the one hand, applying the skill of grasping to new and different objects *does* involve the subsumption of those objects under a pre-existing schema of motor operations. This is what Piaget means by as-

26. Ibid., 75–76.

27. Mencken, "The Divine Afflatus," 158.

28. Piaget, *Intelligence*, 7; see also the lengthy discussion of adaptation and many examples thereof in Piaget, *Origins*, 47–152.

similation. In this regard, Moltmann is right that, to some extent, the intentions of the subject are imposed on the object and the object is available to the subject for this imposition by reason of its similarity (or, I might prefer, "proportion") to the subject as a "grasper." This is, within the dialectic of adaptation, the principle of similarity at work. On the other hand, *success* in applying an old skill to new objects *also* involves the accommodation of the pre-existing schema to the concrete difference(s) encountered in the object. We have to learn, in other words, how to hold spoons differently from baseballs differently from steering wheels, because these things differ both from one another and in proportion to the basic grasping reflex we are born with. This learning means re-coordinating or, as Piaget calls it, "differentiating," the general operational schemata that falls under the name "grasping." The more differentiated our skill at grasping is, the more mobility it has, which is to say the more expansive its world of proportionate objects. Thus, the principle of difference is *also* operative in the development of our prehensile dexterity.

In prehension, then, the application of a basic grasping reflex progressively dilates its horizon of proportionate objects by accommodating itself to those objects through differentiation. This process of differentiation, however, always begins from the base of operational coordination that has thereto been established, and so the requirement of assimilation imposes limits on how far and fast that process can go. Nonetheless, the spontaneous structure of prehensile coordination can, by this process, be rather imaginatively decentralized, as when we learn difficult and relatively "unnatural" manual co-ordinations in order to, for example, play musical instruments or operate delicate tools. As perceptual objectivity was developed by literally looking at objects from more than one angle, so prehensile objectivity is developed by learning lots of subtly different ways of grasping what is proportionate to our fingers and hands.

Thus it is through a back and forth between assimilation and accommodation that the world of objects that are practically meaningful for the subject is progressively unveiled. This expansion, however, is only remotely analogous with the enlargement of a visual horizon. When a visual horizon is expanded, by the removal of impediments or taking a higher vantage, the increase is given all together. It floods in, as it were. The horizon of the graspable, by contrast, is larger the more differentiated our skill at grasping is. This, again, is Piaget's notion of mobility at work. The more mobility a skill like grasping has, the more different objects (or better, the more different *classes* of objects) it can act upon. There are available to me as many classes of graspable objects as there are different ways of grasping in my prehensile repertoire. And so, unlike the dilation of a visual horizon, the expansion of a prehensile horizon is affected, not through greater generality, but through greater *specificity* and through sensitivity to *particularity*. And so under this aspect (and against the characterization offered by Moltmann), difference is primary in the enlargement of the world of the grasp.

REASON AS AP/PREHENSION

Lastly, I want to make good on the promise implied by my title and say something about how knowing is and is not like getting a grip. Both seeing and grasping can, for Piaget, only approach (to adapt the words of Douglas Adams) something not quite entirely unlike objectivity.[29] Insofar as either one transcends the distortions and limitations generated by a relative location in time and space (as in perception) or relative development (as in more or less dexterous prehension), both can make the world available to the subject with greater and greater accuracy, constancy, detail, and reliability. Perception and prehension achieve this almost-objectivity by actively (and eventually habitually) decentralizing the subject's relative location and generalizing beyond the subject's as-yet-achieved development. On Piaget's view, intelligence achieves the proper objectivity denied to either perception or prehension by at once developing in continuity with this process of decentralization and generalization *and* transcending its limits to achieve complete mobility and reversibility. In other words, we could not know without our body, but our knowing is not, in the final analysis, limited by our spatial or temporal location.

We have seen, then, how the development of our grasping skill can be analyzed as a dialectic of active assimilation and passive accommodation. This dialectic expands and refines the efficacy of a basic, hereditary structure. Following Piaget's lead (but diverging somewhat from his emphasis on logic), I will argue that human knowing develops in an analogous fashion. This will allow me to meet the two criteria set above: give an account of cognition that is in continuity with our embodied engagement with things and yet also irreducible to it. To do so, I will appeal to (and, in many ways,

---

29. "(Arthur) had found a Nutri-Matic machine which had provided him with a plastic cup filled with a liquid that was almost, but not quite, entirely unlike tea. . . Arthur drank the liquid and found it reviving," (Adams, *Hitchhiker's Guide to the Galaxy*, 83).

creatively re-present) Catholic philosopher and theologian Bernard Lonergan's philosophy of knowledge.[30] Lonergan's epistemology begins from a model of cognition that consists, like Piaget's model of the grasp, in a core of coordinated operations.[31] These operations, of course, consist not of moving fingers, but acts of intentionality. The horizon of this basic cognitional skill is cumulatively and progressively expanded (that is, in Piaget's terms, granted greater mobility) through differentiation. Moreover, that differentiation is accomplished through a process formally identical with assimilation and accommodation.

For Lonergan, knowing involves the proper coordination of various intentional acts.[32] A primary group of such operations is experiential; it involves granting one's attention in sensation and imagination. In order to know, one has to pay attention to the world of things to be known as it gives itself. But merely paying attention is not yet knowing. As William James argued so fluently, we experience all kinds of things that never make it into the world of our thoughts.[33] One has to also interrogate one's experience. "What was that sound?" "Why is the moon thus darkened?" "What does that word mean?" And these questions call for answers by gaining some insight into what was experienced: "Oh, just the cat again." "The earth has passed between the moon and the sun." And so on. But having a bright

30. Lonergan himself became aware of Piaget's research sometime not long after the publication of his major philosophical work, *Insight: A Study of Human Understanding* in 1957. In a series of lectures on education now edited for the Collected Works, an entire chapter is devoted to Piaget's notions of adaptation and practical intelligence. Lonergan explicitly notes the strength of a position in which objectivity is approached through progressively more adequate construction. See Lonergan, "Piaget and the Idea of General Education," 193–207.

31. It is worth nothing here that operation is a technical term for a single element of a structured activity. "A single (intellectual) operation could not be an operation, because the peculiarity of operations is that they form systems." See Piaget, *Intelligence*, 35–42 on "The Functional Meaning and Structure of 'Grouping.'" See also Piaget's dense and technical 1975 work focusing on cognitional development, *Equilibration of Cognitive Structures*, especially Part II on "The Construction of Structures" and Lonergan's discussion of "formally dynamic structures" in the first *Collection* volume.

32. For Lonergan's terse, but more fully developed account of these intentional acts, the groups into which they coalesce, and the inter-relation of the groups, see section 2 of Chapter 1 in *Method in Theology* (Lonergan, *Method*, 6–13).

33. "Consciousness then does not appear to itself chopped up in bits. Such words as 'chain' or 'train' do not describe it as fitly as it presents itself in the first instance. It is nothing jointed; it flows. A 'river or a 'stream' are the metaphors by which it is most naturally described. *In talking of it hereafter, let us call it the stream of thought, of consciousness, or of subjective life,*" (James, *Psychology: The Briefer Course,* 26).

idea is not yet knowing either. Subsequent to those acts that inquire and offer promising answers, distinct operations are necessary that reflect on the truth, falsehood, probability, or improbability of my bright ideas. Properly speaking, I do not yet claim to know until I judge, "yes" or "no," that my understanding is the *correct* understanding.[34] Knowing is a process, then, but also an accomplishment.

The analogy, then, compares the core scheme of operations in grasping and the core scheme of operations in knowing. Perhaps, however, Lonergan's model of the core cognitional scheme is not yet sufficiently clear. Allow me to illustrate it via a rather different image. The basic or core structure of human knowing is a coordination of operations, a structure of activities something like baking. As one sets out to bake because one wants baked goods generally, and, say, cookies specifically, so also one sets out inquiring because one wants to know in general, and wants to know *this* specifically. As baking consists of measuring, mixing, cooking and cooling, also knowing consists of experiencing, inquiring, understanding, and reflecting or judging. And as in baking, not only do you need all the activities to achieve your object (whether cookies or knowledge), but they must also be related to one another in the proper order. If you do not have ingredients, you are not ready to measure. If you have not measured them, you are not ready to mix them. And, obviously, putting unmixed ingredients (no matter how carefully measured) into a hot oven will not render cookies. Along the same lines, questions are about one's experience, and understandings are answers to those questions. Judgments are about the correctness of one's understandings, one's answers. One has knowledge when one has performed the activities successfully, in their proper coordination, and arrived at a judgment about the correctness of one's understanding(s) because that is what is meant by knowledge. Such, then, is the core skill to be generalized and differentiated in the expansion of human knowledge.

34. It is important to note that, for Lonergan (following Thomas Aquinas), understanding and judging are distinct acts with distinct objects. Rather than the Kantian notion of judgment, in which one combines subject and predicate with the affirmative copula, "is," Lonergan's Thomist notion of judgment is an affirmation of the correctness of an act of understanding or "insight." This distinction of acts is important insofar as it allows true judgments about a being to be apprehensive of some aspects or facets of that being, without claiming to be a totalizing *comprehension* thereof. For Lonergan's full position on true judgments, see Chapters 9–13 of *Insight*. For the roots of this position in Thomas Aquinas, see Chapter 2 of his earlier work, *Verbum: Word and Idea in Aquinas*, 60–105.

So much for the central cognitional structure in Lonergan. What of its expansion via adaptation? How does that aspect of the analogy play out? For Lonergan, the horizon of human knowing is enlarged through differentiations of that skill or structure.[35] The emergence of philosophical inquiry and construction on the Mediterranean opened up onto a whole class of ideas that aspired to being true, not just within the common sense of Athens, but always and everywhere. We see in the writings of Plato the pursuit of the *omni et soli* definition, and in Aristotle the dialectical winnowing of common opinion down to the rigors of a theoretical system. A whole new class of intentional objects could be employed and deployed because a *differentiated* coordination of experience, inquiry, understanding, and judgment had taken hold. The pursuit of adequacy to this new object of knowledge is a better definition of Aristotle's technical appropriation of the Greek word *theoria*.

In the fifteenth and sixteenth centuries, there arose, out of the soil fertilized by the metaphysical quandaries of the thirteenth and fourteenth centuries, differentiations of empirical, scientific study. Western thought began to grapple with, not just universal and necessary structures, but observationally and experimentally verified possibilities. In the eighteenth and nineteenth centuries, the dominant community of Western thought began to interrogate the unique features of human meaning and the requirements of interpreting those meanings across history, as in the then-burgeoning hermeneutical, historical-critical, and sociological scholarship. God knows what the nascent ability to generate and process huge quantities of data will do for the intellectual consciousness for the twenty-first century. These differentiations of our core intellectual scheme precipitated transformations of the Western world, and will no doubt continue to do so.

The hasty genealogy above does not intend to trumpet uncritical praise for all of these developments. I want to be especially explicit that it certainly does not presuppose some notion of inevitable progress. It is meant to express quite the opposite, in fact. It should serve as an illustration of how the basic cognitional structure (pay attention, ask questions, generate answers, check their correctness) has, as a mere matter of contingent

35. Lonergan considers this topic under the heading "Stages of Meaning" and presents them as something like Weber's "ideal types" for the unfolding of Western culture. His model of emerging differentiations (and undifferentiations) of consiousness is more sophisticated than above, but this simplified version will serve to make the more fundamental point about how differentiations transform the world of human understanding. See Lonergan, *Method*, 85–100.

fact, been generalized to assimilate and accommodate a vast array of diverse objects: This or that body of common sense, the rigors of theoretical invariance, the irregularities and complexities of the natural world, the polymorphous multi-verse of human meanings, the immense aggregates of digital technology. The argument, then, is that this expansion has proceeded by a formally identical process to the expansion of the grasp in infancy and childhood. There is a dynamism driving that expansion, but the direction of expansion is indeterminate and its momentum can be interrupted, stalled, or reversed. Nonetheless, human knowledge develops by adaptation through differentiation, and the process of differentiation privileges particularity and relative otherness. Old ways of thinking attempt to assimilate to themselves an ever more general field of beings, but if they are going to be successful, they transform themselves to accommodate those beings in their difference, their particularity. And so alchemy gave way to chemistry.

CONCLUSION

Perhaps it is clear now how the criteria set at the beginning of this essay have been met. On the above model, knowing subsumes both the principle of similarity and the principle of difference in a new context. That new context is the general, dynamic process of emerging adaptation. Our bodily engagement with the world gains in mobility and precision on both an individual and a social level through the dialectic of assimilation and accommodation. Somewhere in the course of our evolution, then, our bodies became the cite emergence for a radically new adaptation: intelligence. Our intelligence is in functional continuity with grasping insofar as it emerges as a mode of world engagement that develops itself through a process of adaptation. It is in functional continuity with our perception insofar as our understandings are sounder with the support of more evidence. Knowing is, however, irreducible to either prehension or perception insofar as it can (in principle) become equal to apprehending objects that are not spatio-temporally available to our bodily locatedness. Our intelligence, resting on the scaffolding of our in our embodiment though it is, may enlarge itself to transcend the limits of perceptual and prehensile relativity in its exploration of the universe. Intelligence, in other words, need not just look or grasp; it may *know*.

Lastly, there are consequences for an expressly *theological* epistemology in this double affirmation of functional continuity and irreducibility between embodied engagement and intellectual knowledge. If human intelligence can be called "spiritual" in its irreducibility, then we might surmise that some kind of knowledge of God, insofar as God is also spirit, is at least and, again, in principle possible for us. Of course, this kind of knowledge would require a unique, "religious," or theological differentiation of intelligent consciousness, and perhaps that differentiation is more or less developed at present than we may think. Nonetheless, such a fittingness of the human mind to the divine mind becomes a plausible object of inquiry. It also suggests that, whatever our Christology may entail, the Incarnation need not be reduced to a mere epistemological aid to hopelessly material creatures. Jesus, in other words, need not merely serve as a picture book lesson for body-addled minds. If our intellectual consciousness is unrestricted in its potential, than perhaps one day the infinite creator of everything will see fit to make our minds concretely and actually adequate to God's self.

BIBLIOGRAPHY

Adams, Douglas. *The Hitchhiker's Guide to the Galaxy*. New York: Gramercy, 2005.

Heidegger, Martin. *Being and Time*. Translated by John Macquarrie and Edward Robinson. New York: HarperCollins, 2008.

James, William. *Psychology: The Briefer Course*. Dover: Courier Dover, 2012.

Lonergan, Bernard. "Cognitional Structure." In *Collection: Papers by Bernard J. F. Lonergan, Volume 4*, edited by Robert M. Doran and Frederick E. Crowe, 1st edition. Toronto: University of Toronto Press, 1993.

———. *Insight: A Study of Human Understanding, Volume 3*. Edited by Frederick E. Crowe and Robert M. Doran. 5th edition. Collected Works of Bernard Lonergan. Toronto: University of Toronto Press, 1992.

———. *Method in Theology*. 2nd edition. Toronto: University of Toronto Press, 1990.

———. "Piaget and the Idea of General Education." In *Topics in Education: The Cincinnati Lectures of 1959 on the Philosophy of Education*, edited by Robert M. Doran, Collected Works of Bernard Lonergan. Toronto: University of Toronto Press, 1988.

———. *Verbum: Word and Idea in Aquinas, Volume 2*. Eited by Frederick E. Crowe and Robert M. Doran. 1st edition. Collected Works of Bernard Lonergan. Toronto: University of Toronto Press, 1997.

Mencken, Henry Louis. "The Divine Afflatus." In *Prejudices: Second Series*. New York: Alfred A. Knopf, 1920.

Moltmann, Jürgen. *The Crucified God: The Cross of Christ as The Foundation and Criticism of Christian Theology*. Translated by R. A Wilson and John Bowden. Minneapolis: Fortress, 1993.

———. *God for a Secular Society: The Public Relevance of Theology*. Translated by Margaret Kohl. Minneapolis: Fortress, 1999.

———. *The Trinity and The Kingdom: The Doctrine of God*. Translated by Margaret Kohl. Minneapolis: Fortress, 1993.

Piaget, Jean. *The Equilibration of Cognitive Structures: The Central Problem of Intellectual Development*. Translated by Terrance Brown and Kishore Julian Thampy. Chicago: University of Chicago Press, 1985.

———. *The Origins of Intelligence in Children*. Translated by Margaret Cook. New York: International Universities Press, 1952.

———. *The Psychology of Intelligence*. Translated by Malcom Piercy. New York: Harcourt Brace, 1950.

CHAPTER 4

Paranoid Perfection

The Body without Organs for the Christian

Matthew Bernico

"But as it is, God arranged the members in the body,
each one of them, as he chose."

—1 Corinthians 12:18

"[W]hile an army of men
descended from a cross,
to which god thought he had long since nailed them,
has revolted,
and, armed with steel,
with blood,
with fire, and with bones,
advances, reviling the Invisible
to have done with God's judgment."

—Antonin Artaud[1]

1. Artaud, "To Have Done With the Judgement of God."

CHRISTIANITY IS A TRADITION of bodily discipline. The performance of liturgy is an apparatus of this discipline—it is a rhythm for the bodily life of the Christian. In worship, there are rules for when one ought to stand, sit, kneel, speak, and sing. However, there is also a secondary discipline of the body outside of worship—a set of normative rules managing the maintenance of the body. These rules determine the relationship of bodies to the Church as well as to other bodies. For example, the Church, following along the trajectory of the Christian tradition, reifies and fixes the use of one's genitals: the penis for reproduction, the vagina for childbirth and so on. That is to say, Christianity shapes and produces certain sexual and nonsexual desires deemed necessary for Christian life. Moreover, in the Wesleyan tradition the bodily discipline that shapes desire is called "holiness," or "perfection." To be self-reflective Christians, then, it is important to inspect this rhythm with rigor.

There is a limited vocabulary for Christians to talk about desire. The Desert Fathers, Augustine, and Aquinas all have something to say about desire, but these thinkers usually look upon desire as something sinful or "of the flesh." For an accurate description of desire in the Christian body, the discussion needs to move beyond the conceptuality and vocabulary of the Church. Due to this vocabulary deficit, one finds Gilles Deleuze and Félix Guattari's framework helpful in understanding Christian desire. Deleuze and Guattari describe a "Body without Organs": a virtual plane of potentialities or a map of desire in the body of individuals. The Body without Organs is a way of speaking about the production of desire in a way that Christianity itself is not capable. Certain theoretical frameworks, such as holiness, already bind Christianity in a rigid matrix that only allows for the practice and reproduction of particular desires. Deleuze and Guattari allow us a line of flight from this rigidity and a method by which we might find new possibilities within Christianity. They lead us to ask: "what is the Body without Organs?," or more simply put, "What kind of desires does Christianity produce?"

The project of this essay is to explore possible desire-producing organs of the Christian body. Since desire is both intimate and communal, this project will lead up to an ecclesial politics and communal ethics. The course for this investigation is threefold: unpacking Deleuze and Guattari's Body without Organs, then tracing an outline of the Body without Organs of the Christian body, and finally, demonstrating the political and ethical repercussions of the Body without Organs of the Christian.

As philosophical terms go, the Body without Organs is probably one of the more abstruse. Difficult or obscure as it may be, it is helpful for diagnosing desire in the Christian body. While the Body without Organs might seem at first as a metaphor, Deleuze and Guattari work to make their definition clear.[2] The BwO is not a metaphor, but deals with the actual bodily existence and reality of entities and whatever they desire. While Deleuze and Guattari work with a number of psychoanalytic terms, they drastically depart from psychoanalysis and, in fact, often strike out against it. Desire, as they conceive it, is rather different from its conception in Freudian or Lacanian psychoanalysis. Moreover, desire, in the sense Deleuze and Guattari use it, is something that one produces rather than something one lacks. This definition opposes Lacan's maxim on desire: "Man's desire is the desire of the Other."[3] Concretely, this difference in the conceptualization of desire concerns one's orientation toward someone or something—that is, one's wanting is produced rather than emerging from absence. Is desire the result of absence or lack? Or rather, is it a positive relation that is generated by some action or orientation? Lacan's model of desire identifies lack or absence as the genesis of desire, whereas Deleuze and Guattari consider desire as something created.

While Lacan's approach is almost purely within the realm of psychoanalysis, Deleuze and Guattari interrogate desire in the realm of politics. They ask the quintessential question of political philosophers after the rise of fascism in Europe: how do the masses come to desire fascism? Desire as positive generation will be explored more thoroughly below; however, one can see the markedly different treatment Deleuze and Guattari offer for mapping out and understanding the topology of desire in what they call desiring-production.

Desiring-production reads like a blueprint for the physical production of desire in the body. The term "blueprint" is especially apt for an explanation of desiring-production, because producing desire means hooking up series of physical mechanisms that produce an array of effects. Deleuze and Guattari begin as simply as possible: "An organ-machine is plugged into an energy-source machine: the one produces a flow that the other interrupts."[4] While remaining abstract, this blueprint outlines the biological, economic and political functions of life. One's organs have a literal power source,

2. From here on out Body without Organs will be abbreviated BwO.

3. Lacan, *Seminar XI*, 235.

4. Deleuze and Guattari, *Anti-Oedipus*, 1.

as do political organs: desiring-production is a means of seeing these connections. For example, glucose, blood and oxygen are all power sources of bodily organs. In an analogous way, we might consider scarcity, security or power as the power sources of political organs. Desiring-production describes the flows of desire as well as the machines and surfaces desire passes through and across. Building on this, Deleuze and Guattari say, "Producing is always something 'grafted onto' the product; and for that reason desiring-production is production of production, just as every machine is a machine connected to another machine."[5] Desiring-production is the production of couplings in order to create desire. Essentially, this formulation brings us to desire as positive production rather than emerging out of negation or lack. This is the means by which ideological, political, economical and religious apparatuses produce desire individuals.

Desire conceived in this way—a positive production—means that desire is produced based on the configurations of organs, energy sources and their connections. Deleuze and Guattari write, "Desire is not bolstered by needs, but rather the contrary; needs are derived from desire: they are counter products within the real that desire produces. Lack is a counter effect of desire; it is deposited, distributed, vacuolized within a real that is natural and social."[6] The order in which one couples or fixes organs determines what desire one's organs will produce and what intensities may flow throughout the body. Once again, to shed light on the rather abstruse language, desire is the result of an assemblage of organs and intensities are the affects that have the possibility for populating these assemblages. For example, certain affects flow in the Christian body that do not flow in the bodies of others. There are certain moralisms that cause the flow of guilt in the body of the Christian. The Christian may feel guilty while passing the homeless on the street, especially if the Christian represses his or her Christ-like desires. The guilt the Christian may feel is the result of certain organizations of organs and the production of desires. In this example, Christianity denotes a particular assemblage of organs and guilt is the intensity that passes through the organs. Deleuze and Guattari estab-

---

5. Ibid., 6.

6. Ibid., 27. My project focuses on desire produced by ideological regimes, but Deleuze and Guattari maintain the capacity to talk about far more than simply ideologies and desire. Both Deleuze and Guattari have written essays on the physical functions of the body elsewhere. There is a lot of interesting insight in their work for those struggling for the rights of disabled bodies as well as those who are gender or sexual minorities. For more on this discourse see Guattari's essay *Becoming-Woman*.

lish a critical orientation toward the fixity of these organs, especially the fixity produced by Freudian Oedipal arrangements. They write, "Oedipus presupposes a fantastic repression of desiring-machines."[7] Freud's Oedipus fixes organs in a particular order and that order produces certain desires and the repression of other desires.

Oedipus may seem distant from our psychological state and so, rather than focus on Oedipus, we can return to the example of the guilty Christian. The conflict and repression of certain desires produce guilt. The Christian tradition demonstrates an obligation to the poor and that obligation generates altruism within Christians, yet other assemblages of organs, which circulate intensities of security, scarcity and accumulation, may repress desires to be altruistic. Clearly, it is more than just Oedipus; all organizations of organs are desire-producing. It is rather a matter of finding beneficial ways of desiring. The enemy is not necessarily any one ideology or orientation, but rather the enemy of the body is the fixity of organs.

Following from this line of exploration, the BwO becomes an increasingly confusing term. The BwO, as Deleuze and Guattari explain, is not opposed to organs, but rather it is opposed to their fixity. "The enemy is the organism. The BwO is opposed not to the organs but to that organization of the organs . . ." Antonin Artaud, the playwright and poet responsible for the term BwO, understands the term as theological in origin. God, at least symbolically, is the enforcer of the order and fixity of the organs.

Artaud's prose may sound devoid of religious possibility. How can there be a Christianity without the fixity imposed by God? It is an interesting statement considering Artaud's biography. In a recent evening lecture at the European Graduate School, Sylvère Lotringer delivered an interesting biographical and philosophical sketch on Artaud and the crisis he observed in the world after WWI.[8] In a general introduction, Lotringer mentioned Artaud's Christianity. He was indeed a Christian, but as Christians know, our relationship to God is often tenuous. Moving forward, one has to observe a certain tension between the continued uses of Artaud's metaphor and Christianity. There is a Christianity on the other side of this analysis, but it is one that resists fixity.

Artaud is a complicated figure and may not contribute to the clarity of the topic. Departing from Artaud, what exactly is the BwO? Deleuze and Guattari begin by explaining that everyone already has one, but it is a

---

7. Ibid., 3.
8. Lotringer, *Antonin Artaud*, European Graduate School, June 13, 2013.

matter of cultivating and playing with it.[9] The BwO is a space for experimentation with the organization of organs and the production of desire.[10] The scope of this experimentation is more than just one's body, "but also biological, and political, incurring censorship and repression."[11] The BwO is a space for new modes or plateaus of life and of desire everywhere. One stretches the BwO with new movements and experimentations in all modes of being. Simply, the BwO is a way to analyze what can be done with our desires, physical bodies, and political bodies. It is interrogating the organizations and the way they normatively operate. Acting in way X is normative, but what else might we do? With the BwO, the body opens up to new connections with the social, political, and natural. In Deleuze and Guattari, we find new anti-teleological possibilities. Deleuze and Guattari lay out a number of possibilities to resist—namely Oedipus and capitalism—but they do not have an end in mind: they invite experimentation.

Perhaps, the most concrete and provocative exposition on the BwO is in Guattari's essay *Becoming-Woman*. *Becoming-Woman* is a proto-queer theory that tries to get at what homosexuality means in the face of heteronormative society as well as the transgressive nature of moving against heteronormativity. According to Guattari, the normative experience of gender is constructed according to phallocratic regimes of power. All gender expressions are developed in their relationship to masculinity and expressions that may fall outside of that relationship are confusing and dangerous to phallocratic power. The homosexual within heteronormative society, as Guattari tells us, is "like a woman" because it does not fit in to the matrix of gender.[12] Phallocratic power relegates non-normative expressions of gender or sexuality to the opposite of masculinity. Homosexuality, transgender, bisexuality and so on are all important ideas in undoing phallocratic power. These expressions of gender and sexuality are important for the discussion of the BwO, because they demonstrate the possible uses and repurposing of one's body. For example, are our genitals fixed? Is the penis destined to forever be phallocratic? What else can we use our bodies for?

All of this theorization of experimentation with desire sounds rather innocuous to a certain extent. Certainly, one can try new things and explore the limit of one's self and body. But the BwO is not a concept, metaphor,

---

9. Deleuze and Guattari, *Thousand Plateuas*, 149.

10. Ibid., 150.

11. Ibid.

12. Guattari, *Becoming-Woman, Hatred of Capitalism*, 356.

or way of self-understanding: it is a real exploration of the possibilities of the body.[13] Exploration is not without possible downfall, failure or mistake. Talking of experimentation, new modes of being sound very exciting, progressive and maybe even joyful. While it can be all of these things, there are real consequences to the BwO. One can botch or ruin the BwO. One can produce desires one did not intend, or new desires may terminate in any number of disastrous avenues. The BwO is not always a good thing; it can lead to a dead end of desire. Deleuze and Guattari note several such botched BwOs one may create. They chronicle the horrors of the botched BwO through the hypochondriac body, the paranoid body, the schizo body, the drugged body and the masochist body.[14] These botched bodies are important to the project of the BwO because they demonstrate an essential principle to experimental bodily practices: caution. Deleuze and Guattari say, "What happened? Were you cautious enough? Not wisdom, caution. In doses. As a rule immanent to experimentation: injections of caution."[15]

Still, how does one make or change one's BwO? One begins with cautious experimentation. This experimentation is a careful orientation toward a new type of desiring and new type of being. Deleuze and Guattari pose it like this, "Where psychoanalysis says, 'Stop, find your self again,' we should say instead, 'Let's go further still, we haven't found our BwO yet, we haven't sufficiently dismantled our self.'"[16] Making a BwO is less about starting from scratch on a new body, but reclaiming the territory of the self and seeing what plateaus are possible. This is what Guattari was describing in *Becoming-Woman*: what possibilities are there when we flee from the phallocratic regimentations of gender?

Reclaiming this territory is rather straightforward. Deleuze and Guattari offer up a program for experimenting with the BwO:

> This is how it should be done: Lodge yourself on a stratum, experiment with the opportunities it offers, find an advantageous place on it, find potential movements of deterritorialization, possible lines of flight, experience them, produce flow conjunctions here

---

13. Ibid., 149.

14. Deleuze and Guattari, *Thousand Plateaus*, 150. I understand the derogatory and ablest connotation that the term "schizo" carries and I strongly empathize with the aversion to the term, however, note that the names for these bodies are the terms Deleuze and Guattari set forth.

15. Ibid.

16. Ibid., 151.

and there, try out continuums of intensities segment by segment, have a small plot of new land at all times.[17]

Deterritorialization is an act of reclamation and liberation: the freeing of a territory from past hegemony. However, a reterritorialization always follows deterritorialization, a space is liberated and turned toward something else. Making a BwO is deterritorializing with caution: "You don't do it with a sledgehammer, you use a very fine file."[18] Making a BwO, therefore, is carefully anti-teleological or at least radically self-determined.

The exact nature of the BwO is determined by what intensities may flow across it. That is the function of the BwO: the possibility for the mediation of certain intensities and the prohibition of others.[19] In this way, the severity of the BwO comes into view. One may end up making a BwO that allows some horrific intensity to pass across it. In the earlier example, guilt was one such intensity that passes across the BwO of the Christian; however, Deleuze and Guattari discuss other extreme types of intensities. For example, Deleuze and Guattari use the possibility of masochistic intensities as an example by interjecting a BDSM program into the text with explicit instructions in regards to the intensities of pain. The masochist creates a BwO, in which the only intensities that may play across the surface of the BwO are the intensities of pain, thus botching or damaging the BwO.[20] One has to ask what intensities can one conduct across one's BwO. Is the BwO already flawed?

As mentioned above, the BwO is a map of desire and potential desire for the individual. Throughout Deleuze and Guattari's collaborative work, their interests were fixed on varieties of BwO. Perhaps, one of the most interesting BwOs that Deleuze and Guattari explain is that of the capitalist. In *Anti-Oedipus*, Deleuze and Guattari state, "Capital is indeed the body without organs of the capitalist, or rather of the capitalist being."[21] As an ideology and set of material conditions, capital now precedes the capitalist. Capitalism becomes an autonomous entity that escapes the control of the capitalist: it is ideology run rampant.[22] While capitalism is an important intersection of Christian life, the BwO this project is interested in is

17. Ibid., 161.

18. Ibid., 160.

19. Ibid., 153.

20. Ibid., 152.

21. Deleuze and Guattari, *Anti-Oedipus*, 10.

22. Bernico, *Capitalism as Body without Organs*, 36.

specifically the BwO of the Christian. In a similar formula, can one say that the BwO of the Christian is Christianity?

Identifying Christianity as the BwO of the Christian seems too broad and unhelpful; Christianity is simply too amorphous and vast to analyze that abstractly. Diagnostically, we ought to be precise by narrowing the scope for greater accuracy. Rather than Christianity as the BwO of the Christian, one needs to map out those organs that shape the desire of the Christian in the Wesleyan tradition. One such organ that creates desire in the Christian body for the Wesleyan tradition is holiness or perfection. Holiness is that fundamental organ that powers the other organs of the church that remain within the Wesleyan constellation. The idea here is not to engage polemically with Wesley or other theologians on holiness, but to examine what kind of desire holiness produces in the body of the church and in the bodies of individuals.

For Wesleyans, holiness is a practice of perfection that relies on God's salvific work. In *A Plain Account of Christian Perfection*, Wesley explains Christian perfection as an orientation of one's heart, mind, and soul toward God.[23] This orientation of organs toward God is perhaps a prototypical understanding of the BwO. The heart, mind, and soul are the necessary organs for Christian life and the proper orientation of these organs is toward God. It is important to note that for Wesley, this perfection is an act of God and not an act of human will. This demonstrates the fixity of the BwO of the Christian. Human perfection or holiness, according to Wesley, requires a rigid production of desires. What type of desire does this produce in the Christian Body?

The coupling of organs that Wesley describes, and the Wesleyan tradition practices, produces a body where only intensities of holiness, justice, love and mercy populate the BwO of the Christian. Yet these intensities are not without flaw or vice. While the Christian BwO can yield a "healthy," but fixed body, it may also produce a botched BwO. The botched or ruined BwO of the Christian is what Deleuze and Guattari outline as the "Paranoid Body." On the paranoid body, Deleuze and Guattari say, "the organs are continually under attack by outside forces, but are also restored by outside energies . . . divine miracles (rays) always restored what had been destroyed." Thus the paranoid body seems all too familiar to the Christian body. Wesley himself demonstrates Christian paranoia in saying:

23. Wesley, *Plain Account of Christian Perfection*.

> Instantly I resolved to dedicate all my life to God, all my thoughts,
> and words, and actions; being thoroughly convinced, there was
> no medium; but that every part of my life (not some only) must
> either be a sacrifice to God, or myself, that is, in effect, to the devil.
> Can any serious person doubt of this, or find a medium between
> serving God and serving the devil?[24]

In this bodily configuration of holiness or perfection one can see the paranoia Deleuze and Guattari disclose. The organs are under attack by temptation, the self, which is also to say the devil. Even more, the antidote for such
a struggle is another outside and cosmic force, God.

Deleuze and Guattari pick up paranoia early on in their project from
one of Freud's cases on a paranoid schizophrenic, Daniel Paul Schreber.[25]
Freud categorizes paranoia with a strong relation to narcissism and within
the locus of the overall Oedipal framework. Explicitly explaining paranoia,
Freud says it is a delusion in which one believes one is being watched.[26] The
paranoiac's belief in being watched and criticized by others as well as the
self is true. Very simply, one is always being observed and watched by one's
peers and one's self; however, the difference between the "healthy" individual and the paranoiac is that the paranoiac is delusional and over-approx-
imates this observation. One is not just receiving criticism from peers or
the super-ego, but directly from God, the devil or any other configuration
of deities. Deleuze and Guattari appropriate and overturn Freud's analysis of Schreber and paranoia throughout *Anti-Oedipus*, reclaiming it from
Freud's Oedipal complex. Rather than carrying forward Freud's assumption
about Schreber's body, Deleuze and Guattari consider Schreber's BwO and
try to understand the production of desire in his body. What this means
for paranoia in this diagnosis is that it is something produced by a BwO.
An analysis of the BwO of the Christian will help us uncover the paranoia
produced in the Christian body.

The paranoiac holiness we see in Wesley is a foundation in evangelical
Christianity in the holiness tradition. In liturgy and worship, this paranoia
appears most resolutely. Liturgy, or what more evangelical congregations
homogenously label as worship, demonstrates a paranoid dialectic between
these demonic external forces and restoring external forces. Even in something as straightforward and traditional as the *Book of Common Prayer*,

24. Wesley, *Perfection*.

25. For more on Schreber, see *The Schreber Case*, by Sigmund Freud.

26. Freud, *On Metapsychology*, 90.

these paranoid organs emerge. Starting with a confession, the church body extols their sin and then gains absolution. In confession, flows of sin are the external forces infesting and attacking the body.

Some Wesleyan congregations have moved from liturgical worship toward a more evangelical worship; however, the escape from formal liturgical worship does not escape the diagnosis of paranoia. Evangelical congregations demonstrate this paranoia more concretely in their worship. Specifically, I think to my experiences with evangelical worship in my university's chapel. The lights are turned down low and the congregation chants a praise chorus that invites God, Jesus, or some combination of the two, along with the Holy Spirit, into our hearts or lives. Evangelical worship is paranoiac in the way it incessantly requests divine flows as correctives to the demonic.

Normatively, the church thinks of sin as a transgressive act against God or God's will. However, it appears that sin is less of an act and more of an inward flow into the Christian body. Sin is the external and alien force that decenters one's heart, mind and soul from Godly perfection. The symptom of sin in erupts in the act, but the formulation of sin we see in Wesley looks more like something that is already inhabiting our bodies. According to the Christian, we might say that sin is the BwO of the non-Christian; it is the intensity that necessarily plays across the surface of the BwO when divine flows are absent. The Christian body only gains its perfection with the absolution of sin from God. This absolution proceeds from confession in the liturgy. Upon confession, the presiding clergy, in the place of Christ, assures congregants remission from their sins through Christ. As Wesley tells us, human perfection—that is holiness—can only be attained by the salvific work of Christ.[27]

Paranoia is problematic ethically and politically because it removes moral agency and political action from the realm of human action. Political, economic or ecological injustice, which is to say sin, becomes the result of demonic forces rather than the responsibility of humanity. We could blame corporations or capitalism for the ecological destruction of the planet, but that neglects the power of Satan and in turn the redeeming power of Christ. From here, one can see how apocalyptic scenarios seem attractive, sin is out of the control of humanity and God will come to restore the world. While there is a romantic sort of appeal to this thought, it leaves room for the reproduction and furthering of all injustice.

27. Wesley, *Perfection.*

Paranoia is a strong diagnosis, to be sure, and one might wonder just how extreme this paranoia might be. Yet the church and its congregants operate in daily life not prohibited by paranoia, but encouraged by it. The paranoia that populates the Christian body poses one serious problem for the church itself: the church will be forever reified as a paranoid body. A paranoid Christianity is stable, but not transformative, salvific, but not liberating. The persistence of paranoia in the Christian body only leads toward the reproduction of this type of body. This is fundamentally incompatible with a Christian ethics. Christianity, performed by Christ, is not something fixed, but dynamic.

The worship assemblage demonstrates a sexually charged paranoia in the church. Deleuze and Guattari explain, "The truth is that sexuality is everywhere"—not just in the bedrooms of married folks or the dens of fornicators, but also in "the way a bureaucrat fondles his records, a judge administers justice, a businessman causes money to circulate; the way the bourgeoisie fucks the proletariat" and, I might add, the way Christians worship God.[28] Christianity, at its base, is a religion that springs from phallocratic foundations; it is an ideological formation that is always asking for penetration in a repetitious way. Phallocentrism in Christianity, or any religion, is difficult. Christianity erupts in the midst of all manner of power structures and historical conditions, patriarchy included. To continue Christianity while discontinuing a historical condition requires a weak break with tradition and a queering of Christianity.[29] Christians need to confront what it means to maintain Christianity in light of this phallocentrism and paranoia. Are these ideological assemblages essential to Christianity?

The resurrection of Christ reveals something transformative, liberating and dynamic. The essential problem this project tries to identify is that Christians have made for themselves a flawed BwO. The BwO of the Christian cannot be something as stable yet paranoid as holiness or perfection. The BwO must be the embodied Christ. While Christ is the embodiment of perfection, it is not the manifestation of perfection we see in Wesley or in evangelicalism. The perfection of Christ is something far more dynamic, wild and prophetic than the evangelical variety. After all, the resurrection

---

28. Deleuze and Guattari, *Anti-Oedipus*, 293.

29. Of course, moving Christianity in new directions requires the voices from a multiplicity of perspectives, though as a cisgendered individual it is beyond my capacity to take the conversation much further.

event alters Christ's body: Christ rises with a wounded body, not something often identified with perfection. This is the perfection of love, not of holiness. The wounded body of Christ speaks to the type of perfection that accompanies messianic power: its strength is in its weakness and liberation in love. Moving from this diagnosis, this project tries to rethink, remap and experiment with the BwO of Christianity. This is a transition in the way Christians desire: a move from holiness toward something a bit more radical.

In order to escape the reproduction of a flawed BwO, the Christian must carefully find lines of flight toward a different configuration of desire-producing organs. This reordering of desiring-production for a new BwO is a matter of ecclesial ethics and politics. Becoming a Christian means falling under the discipline of the church body, but this could be a mistake. Christians should leave this paranoia behind for a different plateau of becoming: a becoming-Christ. Becoming-Christ is not a move of discipline, but of transfiguration or radical theosis. Radical theosis is a means by which one can participate in the immanent spirit of Christ and the Holy Spirit that persists and intermingles with Christian communities since the resurrection. This is not a paranoia, but participation that picks back up the project of Christ ethically and politically.

At first, this might sound like a familiar heresy: the Brethren of the Free Spirit or Marguerite Porete's *Mirror*.[30] In many ways, becoming-Christ is similar in procedure and practice, though I would note some differences between this approach and the medieval mysticism of France or Germany. Certainly, Porete's program for theosis is an exercise in a new mode of desiring. Simon Critchley masterfully outlines Porete's seven steps for theosis or auto-theism: 1.) Being touched by God's grace. 2.) Obeying God's commands and divine law. 3.) The subject undergoes a detachment from the will of the self. 4.) The "decreation" of subject. 5.) Acknowledging the gap between the subject's will and the divine will. 6.) The self that one has "hewn away" becomes the eternal reflection of God. 7.) When one dies bodily, one assume eternal glory.[31] Porete moves from the authority and discipline of the church toward something more radical. The proposals for new theological and ethical relationships that exclude former authority guarantee a heretical label.

---

30. For more on this discourse, see Simon Critchley's *Faith of the Faithless* or Raoul Vaneigem's *Movement of the Free Spirit*.

31. Critchley, *Faith of the Faithless*, 125–29.

However, a sort of masochism remains in the deterritorialization and reterritorialization of Porete's theosis and BwO. Maybe Porete demonstrates the necessity of caution in deterritorialization of desire and the body. Porete's idea of decreation or what Simon Critchley calls self-annihilation is a trope found across a number mystical traditions. However, I remain skeptical about this type of violence toward oneself and what the exact result is, it may be wise to yield to Deleuze and Guattari's caution here: decreation is necessary for any new becoming, but we must remain cautious. Porete hypothesizes that when remove so much of ourselves in decreation, we reflect God. Though, rather than focusing on the self-reflection of God, what if we were to reflect Christ? The reflection of Christ rather than God may seem inconsequential since Christ is God, but the point is that in Christ on finds a human praxis performed by the embodiment of God. Becoming-Christ is an ethical practice that takes up the demands and invitations of Christ.

Christ is the BwO that lurks throughout Christianity; it is that impulse that might be responsible for any good desires in the Christian body. The BwO of Christ is already obvious and available in the narrative of the gospel. Even when Christ is nailed down in the ultimate move of fixity, Christ reorders his body for sustained life and meaning. Christ revolts from this fixity by coming down off the cross and even resisting death. Becoming-Christ is a participation in the continual coming of Christ. This may be a difficult move for the Christian: it is a shift from the wide varieties of apocalyptic thought toward an immanent and materialist understanding of Christ and the gospel.

Becoming-Christ is the rejection of a second coming. Rather, it is the practice and participation in innumerable comings of Christ: this is a re-visitation of realized eschatology. Christianity began as an apocalyptic religion waiting for the second coming of Christ, but this second coming is illusory. There is no second coming, but just participation in the project of Christ. How can one understand the Christ event in any finitude? Christ is always coming in those who practice love in his way. This is understanding the term Christ and the idea of the messiah in a particularly interesting and abstract way. One may see the rupture of Christ in the person of Jesus, but one may also see it among others.[32] Practicing this plateau is practicing a

---

32. This potentially puts my project in a tough place. To what extent is Christ a unique rupture in human history and what can one make of others practicing Becoming-Christ? On material terms, one can at least say that Becoming-Christ is a practice and the historical person of Jesus is the archetypal figure for this practice. However, the Christian tradition urges one to say more about the person of Jesus.

type of liberation that we see in the person of Jesus. This is not the liberation from one political economy to another, but to another world and another logic of social and theological relations. Then, precisely what does it mean to participate in Becoming-Christ? Simply, in all things act in wasteful love: scarcity cannot exist in the economy of Christ.

Perhaps, one can say that this practice is learning to negotiate, but overall reject Paul's eschatological vision of the kingdom that is already, but not yet. Becoming-Christ is an attempt at bridging the gap between the kingdom of God and the world as it is. The "not yet" is untenable in contemporary political economy, but the world desperately needs transformation in the way of Christ. Overall, life is too precarious and oppression too rampant to wait for a cosmic messianic event: we need love and liberation today. Becoming-Christ is the possibility for a rupture in the current state of things and the breaking in of a new world. This rupture is the space for politics and ethics: oligarchic pseudo-democracies and free-market economics are just business as usual, politics happen in ruptures, rebellion against, and destruction of these systems. Practicing this becoming is possibly revolutionary, or at least not kind to current regimes of oppression. Becoming-Christ is not necessarily a Marxist endeavor, although it does have communist repercussions. It is not the revolution of class against class, but the power of love against evil.[33] Becoming-Christ practices love that liberates class through the power of love. This is not the hatred of one class over another, but an indignation and yearning for liberation and justice. This does not mean class or any other socio-economic factors are not important; rather, Becoming-Christ is the abolition of worldly boundaries through love. This point requires some careful navigating, as one must still consider the intersectional identities of race, gender, sexuality and class. Becoming-Christ is not a liberal scheme to become "color blind" or tolerant. Rather, it is a therapy and a reorientation toward the other.

Practicing this becoming is what Michael Hardt and Antonio Negri call alter-modern. This is an adopted and reworked idea taken from Hardt and Negri's *Commonwealth*.[34] Briefly, Christianity cannot exist in in movements of pure resistance or pure acceptance and acquiescence. The project found in Becoming-Christ is similar to that found in the slogans of the

33. It is not my intention to exclude Marxist theory from the discussion; in fact, much of the underlying thought used here is Marxist in origin. It is simply that Marxism is not sufficient for this critique and negotiation of Christian *praxis*.

34. Hardt and Negri, *Commonwealth*, 67.

Zapatistas: "Another world is possible." Pairing Becoming-Christ with any political economy or structure of power does not seem to work. It is not so simple as to say Becoming-Christ is a communist, socialist, capitalist, or anarchist practice. Surely, one may find the trace of these different political economies within Becoming-Christ. However, it is beyond the capacity of these projects to speak to the alter-modern kingdom of God. In practicing this mode of life, one must find new methods managing the commons and labor. How can one practice the emulation of Christ amongst exchange relations and property? In the Christian narrative, Christ does not demand payment for his life and our salvation, but invites all into a new world. How can we put together capitalist economies with a way of life that Christ offers freely? Christ's death dissolves property.

The Eucharist is the best example of how Christ reimagines property, scarcity and love. When Christ invites one to the table for Eucharist, one freely receives Christ's body and blood. The reception of Eucharist cannot exist in the paradigm of capitalist exchange relations. In the capitalist political economy, Christ comes off as crazy or at least a bad businessman. One will not increase profits by practicing the business model of Christ. In fact, in Christ's giving of his body we see private property for what it is: the result of sin and alienation. The original sin in the garden is the result of a lack of faith or trust in God and it results in the alienation from God and our fellow humans. Out of alienation arises the impulse to security and fear: this alienation is the genesis of private property. Alienation is the opposite of love: when we are transformed through love, various arrangements of market economies cannot hold.

Overall, this thought follows from perhaps an abuse of another philosopher of desire, Raoul Vaneigem. Vaneigem speaks on desire from quite a different register than Deleuze and Guattari. Vaneigem, focusing on desire, talks about what he calls the alchemy of the self.[35] Alchemy is the process of the transmutation of elementary forms of life into human life. I see an advanced alchemy within the Eucharist; it takes the human life and transforms it through love. Eucharist is a free and wasteful love: just anyone can receive it. Even more, Eucharist is an important practice for Becoming-Christ, because it is a learned practice that shapes desire: it is connecting individual bodies to Christ's body. As Jesus offers up his body and blood for all of us, one who practices Becoming-Christ must do the same. This is not the call for mass-martyrdom, but simply for a type of love that exceeds the

35. Vaneigem, *Movement of the Free Spirit*, 236.

capacity of capitalist and socialist relations. Practically, becoming-Christ means giving our body and blood, a meal, our labor, our creativity to our own beloved communities.

Christianity produces a BwO of the Christian that is flawed with paranoid desire. Being a Christian is not enough, discipline certainly has its place, but to take up the transformative project of Christ, Christians need to rethink desire and in turn ethics. Becoming-Christ lets us repurpose our paranoid bodies into organizations with new potentialities. The kingdom of God is amongst this type of becoming. Resurrect the paranoid bodies fixed stiffly in religiosity, consumption, struggle and accumulation with the reordering of the body and the reorienting power of love.

BIBLIOGRAPHY

Artaud, Antonin: *To Have Done With the Judgement of God.* http://www.surrealism-plays. com/Artaud.html.

Bernico, Matt. *Capitalism as Body without Organs: An Autonomist Account of Capital.* MA thesis, University of Illinois in Springfield, 2013.

Critchley, Simon. *The Faith of the Faithless: Experiments in Political Theology.* Brooklyn: Verso, 2014.

Deleuze, Gilles, and Félix Guattari. *Anti-Oedipus: Capitalism and Schizophrenia.* Minneapolis: University of Minnesota Press, 1983.

Lacan, Jacques. *Seminar XI: The four fundamental concepts of psycho-analysis.* New York: Norton, 1998, 1973.

Lotringer, Sylvère, *Antonin Artaud,* European Graduate School, June 13, 2013.

Negri, Antonio, and Michael Hardt. *Commonwealth.* Cambridge: The Belknap Press of Harvard University Press, 2009.

Vaneigem, Raoul. *The Movement of the Free Spirit: General Considerations and Firsthand Testimony Concerning Some Brief Flowerings of Life in the Middle Ages, the Renaissance, and, Incidentally, Our Own Time.* New York: Zone, 1994.

Wesley, John. "Plain Account of Christian Perfection." Christian Classics Ethereal Library. http://www.ccel.org/ccel/wesley/perfection.ii.iii.html.

Church Bodies

CHAPTER 5

Divine–Human Relationships

A Case for an Embodied God

Joyce Ann Konigsburg

THE GOD OF CHRISTIANITY is a relational God who desires connection and association with creation, especially human beings. In reaching out to humanity, God utilizes theophanies or divine appearances to reveal aspects of God's nature and divine plans and to transform and engage people in meaningful and personal relationships. Human creatures, being part spiritual in nature and also temporal, finite, and corporeal, experience the world through their senses, intellect, and imagination. When relating to or describing God, embodied people employ anthropomorphism, a process of ascribing human characteristics to the divine, even though it presents theological challenges and imposes restrictions on a transcendent deity. Given humanity's limitations and ontological differences with the divine, embodying God within imaginative, anthropomorphic language and other meaningful symbolic representations advances the understanding and significance of divine theophanies and promotes divine–human relationships.

HUMAN NATURE AND LIMITS

The human body orients and mediates a person's knowing, sensing, and being in the world. Embodied by nature, people "correlatively define and are defined by the world" through the use of their physical senses which determine subjectivity and objectivity and establish yet limit human potential.[1] Humans therefore theorize and construct symbols about the abstract, intangible, and transcendent using their senses, intellect, and imagination. Even one's imagination is "caught within the confines of the limits of our embodiment" and is also linguistic, historic, contingent, time–bound, contextually–based, so as a result, "we cannot imagine just anything" without it having some basis in reality.[2] When people develop initial images of God, they employ early childhood feelings, memories, prayer experiences, and narratives within lived cultural and social contexts.

These images of God are frequently anthropomorphic or possessing a human form. Anthropomorphism is a creative, essential, yet involuntary response motivated by the human need to explain, understand, and predict the behavior of real or imagined non-human agents including God, the boogeyman, hurricanes, and computers.[3] Psychologists think anthropomorphic practices "help us to simplify and make more sense out of complicated entities" and to cope when "ultimate reality is imagined to be beyond our ability to grasp."[4] Assigning human traits and personalities to non–human entities also grants them moral value, a pseudo–identity, and respect. This personification promotes interaction and establishes interpersonal connections since the "self" exists in and is defined through associations with "others."

Human beings participate in both divine and person–to–person relationships; in fact "divine relationships may approximate concrete social relationships in intensity" and satisfaction.[5] Although unable to see, hear, or touch the divine, God is "powerfully present psychologically to the believer," thereby making the relationship real and intense.[6] Faith enables and sustains relationships between the fundamentally different divine

---

1. Nikkel, *Radical Embodiment*, 90.

2. Elshtain, *Augustine and the Limits of Politics*, 58, 60.

3. O'Neill, *Five Bodies*, 3; Guthrie, *Faces in the Clouds*, viii; Epley et al., "On Seeing Human," 864.

4. Nauert, "Why Do We Anthropomorphize?" in Miller, *Three Faces of God*, 86.

5. Pollner, "Divine Relations, Social Relations, and Well-Being," 92.

6. St. Clair, *Human Relationships and the Experience of God*, 19, 24.

and human natures. Nevertheless, this sacred type of affiliation "must be congruent with the capacity for human relationships" and thus requires communication, commitment, trust, and engagement. Anthropomorphism helps people recognize and relate to God more effectively even if the human mind cannot fully comprehend divine transcendence.[7]

THEOLOGICAL CHALLENGES AND MITIGATIONS

Humanity and divinity are two radically different ontological and epistemological categories of being; therefore, divine anthropomorphism poses several significant theological challenges regarding classical notions of God's nature and attributes. Anthropomorphism, for example, contradicts "the historic transcendence and otherness of the Abrahamic God" and it risks "the possibility that God consists *only* in anthropomorphizing;" hence theologians "wish to eliminate anthropomorphism but admit they cannot . . . [because] it is so embedded in their Scriptures."[8] As a case in point, Judeo-Christian texts portray God in human terms with a face, eyes, ears, hands, fingers, and feet that enable the Lord to sit, walk, speak, listen, and act. Moreover, God exhibits intention and expresses love, anger, compassion, justice, and mercy. Using the phrase "then God . . . " even assigns temporal aspects to an eternal being.[9] To minimize anthropomorphism's effects, some theologians analyze and calculate elaborate measurements for God's body parts in so much detail as to render the notion of a divine body ridiculous, illogical, and incongruous.

Anthropomorphic deities nevertheless reflect the reality of human experience and the thoughts of influential Christian theologians. St. Augustine believes God to be a material substance or "a vast and bright body."[10] Although St. Thomas Aquinas "never alleges that God is in any way embodied, he does equivalently talk about divine omnipresence" and understands that "the root of the belief in God's corporeality is our inability to imagine God without using corporeal images."[11] As ideas about God's essence changed, early Christian Church fathers attempted "to reconcile Biblical anthropomorphism with the platonic conception of spirit

---

7. Ibid., 3.

8. Guthrie, *Faces in the Clouds*, 179, 180.

9. Barrett and Keil, "Conceptualizing a Nonnatural Entity," 221.

10. St. Augustine, *Confessions* IV, 36.

11. Dombrowski, "Does God Have a Body?" 227; Wainwright, "God's Body," 470.

as immaterial, ideal, and absolute. Like Maimonides, they found human attributes incompatible with [divine] mystery and majesty."[12]

Furthermore, the necessity of using anthropomorphic images when referencing the divine prompted the art of iconography based on descriptions of God in Scriptures. One of the outcomes from the iconoclastic controversies of eighth century Christianity demonstrates that without tangible reminders of religious persons and events, people have difficulty relating to abstract views of God. St. John of Damascus defends the use of holy icons and religious images as helping people remember past events while pointing to future promises. Setting aside political and cultural aspects, the theological controversy involved several Christological heresies and arguments about idolatry. The iconoclasts feared icons violated God's commandments against graven images and that people would worship the icons rather than God. St. John of Damascus rejects depicting the transcendent God as an image although justifies icons of Jesus, Mary, and the saints by claiming that Christ's incarnation, as the true image of the invisible Father, alters the meaning of Old Testament laws. Furthermore, an icon is not the same essence as what it images. People do not revere the icon *per se* but the subject of the icon itself. Veneration of the icon is not the same as worship; adoration is reserved for God. These arguments mitigated concerns and contradictions that involved worshiping icons and limiting an almighty and all-powerful transcendent God to anthropomorphic concepts and representations.

The Ancient Near East and Mediterranean religions believed their gods to be "transcendently anthropomorphic," meaning that the gods' bodies "possessed a form of human shape but of divine substance and quality."[13] Many Egyptian and local area gods are depicted as having bodies the color of dark blue lapis lazuli, considered to be a divine substance and an ancient reference to sapphire.[14] Employing some of these ideas, Priestly sources of the Hebrew Bible describe YHWH as a singular "body" being different in substance, unknown in size, yet similar only in form to humanity, therefore, the God of Israel was probably conceptualized as "transcendently anthropomorphic; that is to say, he [sic] possessed a body so sublime it bordered on the non–body," a body quite possibly blue in color.[15] The Priestly method

12. Guthrie, *Faces in the Clouds*, 181.

13. Williams, "Sapphiric God," 4.

14. Ibid.

15. Ibid., 6.

of representing YHWH's image uses the concept, Glory of God (*kāvôd*), which is "symbolism grounded in mythological corporeal imagery."[16] God's "bodily" presence appears in one place at any given time and eventually transcends earth to enter heaven. Deuteronomic sources counter notions of the divine Glory with a theology involving the divine Name (*shem*) as an abstraction or a sign that represents God, except it points to the divine residing in heaven rather than God's actual presence in the Temple. The resulting dialectic between hearing the Name (theo-aural) and seeing the Glory (theo-phanic) provides counterbalance between transcendence and immanence, increases ambiguity and mystery, and diminishes divine anthropomorphism.[17]

Elohist biblical sources substitute dreams and angelophanies to mitigate the anthropomorphism of God. Dreams are not tangible or verifiable so they offer a vague, alternate reality when encountering God's presence. Even though communication may occur at a subconscious level, it is not as transforming for a person as is a direct theophanic experience. Angels provide a more substantive experience as distinct supernatural messengers sent by God. As the Lord's ambassadors, angels alternatively act with divine authority and perform anthropomorphic tasks instead of God.[18] Though angels often are portrayed as "the subject rather than as a substitute" in redacted narratives, angelophanies mediate knowledge of God and substitute for the divine form during human encounters.[19] Angelophanies consequently act as a filter through which God may be seen, revealed, encountered, and experienced, but not completely understood.

In other parts of Scripture, Wisdom also mediates divine-human relationships because "the reflection of God's presence through Wisdom remains nonetheless an indirect form of contact with God and a reminder of the limits of human perception and understanding."[20] Wisdom itself is an embodied pre-existent figure assisting God at creation (Wis 8:22–31) and possessing many roles "including teacher, prophet, desirable woman, wife, artisan, and even Goddess."[21] Moreover, the literature of Job and Ec-

16. Orlov, "Praxis of the Voice," 58.

17. Ibid., 60; Terrien, *Elusive Presence*, 142–52.

18. von Heijne, *The Messenger of the Lord in Early Jewish Interpretations of Genesis*, 118.

19. Barr, "Theophany and Anthropomorphism in the Old Testament," 33; Miller, *Three Faces of God*, 86.

20. Burnett, *Where Is God? Divine Absence in the Hebrew Bible*, 104.

21. Ibid., 103.

clesiastes portray the embodiment of God's Wisdom through justice and an orderly cosmos for "the world's moral and natural order provides the chief evidence of God's presence."[22]

Another way to alleviate problems with anthropomorphism is to claim it is metaphorical. St. Clement, for example, rejects any human form or emotions as being associated with the nature of God and considers "biblical ascriptions are metaphors adapted to the limitations of human understanding;" hence he believes that out of reverence, one should not think literally about bodies or figures "and *motion* or *standing* or *seating*, [*sic*] or *place*, or *right* or *left* as pertaining to the Father of the universe."[23] Other theologians accept that natural elements present physical, yet metaphorical, manifestations the divine using recognizable items such as burning bushes, rocks, pillars of fire, smoke, lightning and thunder, whirlwinds, and especially clouds. A cloud covers the tent of meeting as God's Glory enters the tabernacle thereby representing God's presence and likewise, the Son of Man is seen coming on clouds.[24] In fact, "the act of coming with clouds suggests a theophany of Yahweh [*sic*] himself."[25] The cloud image also "is rooted in the ancient tradition of describing God as wrapped in a cloak of clouds or light."[26] Jewish, Samaritan, Christian, and Gnostic literature utilize the term "garment" or cloak as a metaphor for the body and the body in turn is the soul's garment.[27] In a similar fashion, the high priest revealed "God's visible presence" by wearing richly adorned temple vestments, which represent "the body or skin of the deity."[28] When performing his cultic duties, the high priest became analogous to "the Logos in the cosmic temple" while the temple vestments, veils, and drapes "symbolized the material body of the immanent Logos," their colors representing the four natural elements.[29]

Notions of fragmentation and fluidity in Ancient Near Eastern religions contend that a deity is simultaneously present and independent in multiple bodies (objects) or places either as several manifestations of a single god that are identical to yet also distinct from each other, or different

---

22. Ibid., 105.

23. Ibid., italics original.

24. Dan 7:13; Matt 24:30, 26:64; Mark 13:26, 14:62.

25. Boyarin, *Jewish Gospels*, 40.

26. Williams, "Sapphiric God," 16n127.

27. Ibid., 15.

28. Ibid., 8, 15.

29. Ibid., 21, Exod 26–28.

gods that are various aspects of a single deity.[30] The gods' physical and ontological attributes thus are radically different from humans who possess one unique body and self. In the Hebrew Bible, mention of natural elements such as burning bushes, rocks, pillars of fire, clouds, etc., while interpreted as metaphorical representations of the divine, also may serve as divine fragments of the one God. Jewish mysticism additionally supports divine fragmentation in relationship or "intradeical dynamism," but considers each holy fragment as part of a unified whole which is God.[31] Humanly constructed items also incorporate God; worship in "the Temple as the anthropomorphic body of God" recognizes that various holy areas of the sanctuary "correspond to degrees of divine presence."[32]

An all–encompassing metaphor for the embodiment of God is the concept of panentheism, which attempts to reconcile concerns between divine transcendence and immanence. Although experiencing a resurgence of interest, the concept of the world as God's body dates back to Stoicism and Platonism, with early Christian theologians Tertullian and Irenaeus contemplating the idea.[33] Panentheism is extremely careful to distinguish between the divine and the world in order to retain ontological differences and distance God's association with imperfection, evil, suffering, and physical limitations. The Platonic model upholds panentheism without sacrificing classical theology by suggesting that "the soul creates or produces or emanates its own body . . . [as] an image or expression of the soul (or higher self)."[34] Eschatological or Soteriological panentheism claims that "only when creation reaches final perfection it is said to reside 'in God.'"[35] St. Augustine would agree with Eschatological or Soteriological panentheism because he believes visions of the divine occur only after death or at the Eschaton. He concedes that created matter as metaphors and supernatural intercessors are instruments of communication that mediate God's presence; they are mediating instruments or theophanies of revelation; thus St. Augustine avoids direct anthropomorphism and alternative appearances of the divine while reaffirming God's transcendence.

---

30. Sommer, *Bodies of God and the World of Ancient Israel*, 14–16.

31. Ibid., 129.

32. Burnett, *Where Is God*, 124.

33. McFague, "World as God's Body;" Wainwright, "God's Body," 479.

34 Wainwright, "God's Body," 479, 481.

35 Nikkel, *Radical Embodiment*, 138.

THEOPHANIES—DEFINITION AND GOALS

From the Greek word meaning "appearance of God," theophanies are manifestations of the divine in ways available to human perception, generally through the senses and imagination. However, St. Albert the Great associates theophany with human intellect, the former being "an illumination descending from God which allows the created intellect not to see what God is," but to see the divine as God presents and discloses God's self to the intellect and rational reasoning.[36] Whether through human senses, imagination, or intellect, during theophanic encounters, God transforms people, establishes relationships, and reveals divine plans for the world.

Even though theophanies last a short time, a person's first reaction is to hide from such an unusual or uncomfortable religious experience that is meant to be transforming. A religious experience with God produces internal and external changes to one's identity, outlook, and ethics. From their theophanic encounters, Abram, Sarai, and Jacob receive new the new names Abraham, Sarah, and Israel, respectively.[37] After his divine wrestling match, Jacob changes his outlook and ethics from bargaining with God to obedience and acceptance of his promised destiny.[38] Moses gains confidence and assertiveness as a result of his divine encounters and even "implored the Lord" to spare the people their sins in crafting a golden calf.[39] During his forty days on Mount Sinai with God, Moses also transforms physically since "the skin of his face had become radiant when he conversed with the Lord."[40] Through an internalized apocalyptic process, theophanies change people, reinstate their original natures, and prepare them for meaningful relationships with God, others, and themselves.

One effect of theophanic transformation is to become a worthy vessel for God. The Hebrew creation story of the first man, Adam, made in the image of God, parallels Ancient Near Eastern stories involving statues which are "made for/by the deity from mundane materials into which that deity subsequently enters and dwells."[41] A special ritual consecrates and activates the vessel or container; for example, God breathes into the

36. Jones, "Filled with the Visible Theophany of the Lord," 3.

37. Gen 17, 35.

38. Gen 32.

39. Exod 32:11.

40. Exod 34:29.

41. Williams, "Sapphiric God," 13.

three-dimensional clay likeness of God's image and creates Adam and the rest of humanity as living statues revealing divine presence. When people sin, they become broken statutes and are unable to function as full and perfect divine images until transformed by theophanies.[42]

Another manifestation causing transformation and communion with God is *Hesychasm*, a "psychophysical method of prayer" through which "the divine presence is integrated into the rhythm of the body."[43] The practice of being still, peacefully breathing, and concentrating on the holy Name (*shem*) of Jesus, induces a mystical experience of ecstasy upon entering God's presence and seeing the divine light. St. Gregory Palamas, defender of *Hesychasm* in the fourteenth century, clearly distinguishes between the energies of God, which may be seen and experienced, as opposed to God's unknowable essence. During *Hesychasm*, the practitioner is transformed through the grace and energy of the Holy Spirit (*theosis*) and given the ability to experience the energies of God in a visible theophany.[44] The experience of Trinitarian grace "transcends both the senses and the intellect" yet enables the embodied person, to the extent of one's capabilities and finitude, to see energies of the uncreated light and "close the gap between God and creatures," though never completely, for Palamas denies humans can become God by nature.[45]

Theophanies reveal but also conceal God from people unprepared or in need of transformation. Some violations of God's holy presence meant death[46] but most of the time God's Glory is veiled or hidden from sight as from the crowd of people who were afraid of the cloud enveloping the mountain and of a luminous Moses.[47] Mary Magdalene and the disciples at Emmaus initially did not recognize the risen Christ until "their eyes were opened" and they realized the truth.[48] Evidently, divine theophanic encounters remain "forever hidden from our human abilities to grasp" unless given the grace to understand what God reveals.[49]

---

42. Sommer, *Bodies of God*, 22.

43. Nes, *Uncreated Light*, 97.

44. Jones, "Filled with the Visible Theophany of the Lord," 6.

45 Coates, "Bakhtin and Hesychasm," 67; Jones, "Filled with the Visible Theophany of the Lord," 1, 9.

46. Lev 10:1–3.

47. Exod 34:27–35.

48. John 20:14–16; Luke 24:13–32.

49. Nicholas of Cusa, *Vision of God*, 19.

In addition to transformation, theophanic encounters establish and progressively develop relationships between humans and the divine. Images or appearances of God "do not *describe* God but express ways and experiences of relating to God" by utilizing familiar components of lived, human reality.[50] The Lord's association with Abraham, for example, begins using recognizable covenantal or political agreements consisting of promises, conditions, trust, and faithfulness from both parties. However, signs of deeper bonds include Abraham knowing and calling for the Lord by name,[51] God passing between the split halves of sacrifice rather than Abraham, the less powerful covenantal partner,[52] the divine visitors dining and sharing in Abraham's hospitality,[53] and God permitting Abraham to argue and negotiate the fate of Sodom and Gomorrah without condemnation or reproach.[54] On the other hand, Jacob requires physical confrontation for his attitude and character to improve. Eventually, Jacob's relationships with God, Esau, and others are strengthened. And through numerous theophanies, Moses' interactions with God gradually change from uncertainty and non-commitment to a special relationship where the people and the priests must not go up the mountain, for "Moses alone is to come close to the Lord."[55] Furthermore, whenever Moses entered the tent of meeting "the Lord used to speak with Moses face to face" and said to him "you have found favor with me and you are my intimate friend."[56] Because of their unique rapport, Moses asks to see God's Glory but is granted only a view of God's back until Christ's transfiguration when Moses speaks directly to God's Son.[57] With each theophany, God approaches and interacts with people in an appropriate manner and intensity necessary to develop the divine–human relationship and to accomplish God's divine plan.

Theophanies therefore reveal and assist in actualizing God's plans for the world. During divine encounters with Abraham, God discloses future promises of land, descendants, and blessings as well as plans for the

50. McFague, "World as God's Body," italics original.

51. Gen 13:3.

52. Gen 15:9–21.

53. Gen 18.

54. Gen 18:22–33.

55. Exod 19:12–13, 21–25; 24:17, 2.

56. Exod 33:11, 17.

57. Exod 33:18–23; Matt 17; Mark 9; Luke 9.

destruction of Sodom and Gomorrah.[58] In Jacob's dream, God reveals a ladder with angels ascending and descending, reiterates promises made to Abraham, and pledges protection for Jacob on his journeys.[59] The Lord discusses divine intentions of sending Moses to talk with Pharaoh about freeing the Israelites, answers all Moses's questions, and prophesizes about the eventual outcome in Egypt.[60] In chapter 4 of Exodus, Moses still doubts the mission and his abilities, but God patiently instills confidence in Moses, offers Aaron as an assistant, and teaches Moses supernatural signs to perform before Pharaoh. At Mount Sinai, the Lord directly discloses the Ten Commandments and detailed instructions for the ark, the dwelling tent, and cultic rituals and practices. Thus, each theophany is a communication conduit revealing God's promises, plans, and prophesies.

Although veiled and unclear, theophanies foreshadow the incarnation event, the perfect theophany/christophany of God. Christians reading the Hebrew Scriptures interpret theophanies to be christophanies. Early Church fathers reasoned that the Father was invisible yet the Son was visible through the incarnation, so Old Testament appearances were of the Son who therefore must be distinct from the unseen Father. Hence, Jesus is thought to be an angel (angelomorphic Christology) who speaks to Abraham,[61] wrestles with Jacob,[62] and gives the law to Moses on Mount Sinai.[63] As theology progresses, Christ becomes a new category of being; he is the Christ, the Messiah, Son of God, Son of Man, and a reflection of God's Glory. Jesus Christ, through theophanies, connects the Old and New Testaments as the same revelation of the Father.[64] Thus "Christian kerygma is also rooted in the concrete experience of Old Testament theophanies" by employing "Yahweh Christology" expressed in New Testament writings.[65]

The incarnation of Jesus Christ is a special type of theophany for Christ is the presence of God embodied through a hypostasis retaining the integrity of the divine and human natures. Prior to Christ's incarnation, theophanies revealed God, although in enigmatic ways. However, Jesus Christ is a

58. Gen 12, 17.

59. Gen 28.

60. Exod 3.

61. Gen 18.

62. Gen 28.

63. Exod 3, 19.

64. 1 Cor 10:1–5.

65. Bucur, "Exegesis of Biblical Theophanies in Byzantine Hymnography," 97.

tangible, visible presence who perfectly reveals the Father.[66] Because God the Father "is invisible and inaccessible to creatures, it is necessary for those who are going to approach God to have access to the Father through the Son" and likewise, the transcendent God approaches and establishes a relationship with humanity through the tangible, incarnate Son.[67]

In the New Testament, Jesus alludes to his corporal body when he says he will raise the Temple in three days and St. Paul writes that the human body is a temple of the Holy Spirit and is meant to glorify God.[68] Paul also describes the Church as the mystical body of Christ in which a diverse group of people form a visible unified Christian community revealing God to the world.[69] Dionysius teaches that saints in the next life are "filled with the visible theophany of the Lord as the disciples were in the Transfiguration" and thus establishes a connection between theophanies in this life and the beatific vision in the afterlife.[70]

Worship, sacrifice, and memorial services invoke God's divine presence in the hearts and minds of the assembly every time the people call God by name and recall God's past deeds, especially during powerful and liberating acts such as the Exodus and Christ's Last Supper. As a relational God, the divine presence is a presence in and of community, for wherever God is embodied in the gathering of the faithful, God's love is revealed and it subsequently transforms the gathering into a theanthropic community.[71] Christian sacraments utilize audible words, tactile signs and symbols, and kinetic ritual actions in manifesting God's presence and grace to the participants. Each sacramental encounter is a Trinitarian experience, and for some Christians the Eucharist is a special encounter where "the risen Lord is present and acts in the name of the Father and through the Holy Spirit to strengthen the relationships within his body." The Eucharist then is a theophany; the body of Christ is physically and spiritually present to each worthy communicant in the faith community.

---

66. John 1:18, 3:31–32, 5:19–20, 5:36–38.

67. St. Irenaeus of Lyons, *On the Apostolic Teaching*, 71; Eph 2:18–22, 3:12.

68. John 2:19; 1 Cor 6:19–20.

69. 1 Cor 12:4–26.

70. Jones, "Filled with the Visible Theophany of the Lord," 5.

71. FitzGerald, "Holy Eucharist as Theophany," 30.

CONCLUSION

The relational Trinitarian God of Christianity employs theophanies and other forms of manifestation to reveal, transform, and ultimately develop meaningful relationships with humanity. However, due to human nature and its limitations, God's appearances and interactions must engage the human senses, intellect, and imagination to be effective. God may choose anthropomorphic and other tangible forms of theophany in order to establish interpersonal communication and deeper relationships with imperfect, embodied human creatures. This does not suggest that anthropomorphic theophanies result from God's essence nor are they natural or characteristic forms for God. Instead, God tailors divine manifestations to provide an optimum and appropriate religious experience, to customize each person's transformation based on particular circumstances and needs, and to relate in personal, intimate, and unique ways on an individual basis with humanity. People anthropomorphize the incomprehensible transcendent God because doing so helps them connect, associate, and establish trust more rapidly when "the other" shares similar characteristics with themselves.

Anthropomorphism may be theologically incorrect, "but it also is reasonable and inevitable" because humans "remain condemned to meaning, and [for humanity] the greatest meaning has a human face."[72] Yet while imagining, sensing, contemplating, and rationalizing may assist people to comprehend and establish relationships with a loving transcendent God, ultimately "we walk by faith, and not by sight" in communion with the divine.[73]

---

72. Guthrie, *Faces in the Clouds*, 204.

73. 2 Cor 5:7.

BIBLIOGRAPHY

Alexander, Hieromonk. "Dionysius Areopagites in the Works of Saint Gregory Palamas: on the Question of a 'Christological Corrective' and Related Matters." http://www.marquette.edu/maqom/Corrective.html.

Altizer, Thomas J. J. *The Self-Embodiment of God*. Lanham: University Press of America, 1977.

Andresen, Jensine. *Religion in Mind: Cognitive Perspectives on Religious Belief, Ritual, and Experience*. New York: Cambridge University Press, 2001.

Bar-Ilan, Meir. "The Hand of God: A Chapter in Rabbinic Anthropomorphism." http://faculty.biu.ac.il/~barilm/handofgd.html.

Barnes, Michel Rene. "The Visible Christ and the Invisible Trinity: Mt. 5:8 in Augustine's Trinitarian Theology of 400." *Modern Theology* 19:3 (2003) 329–55.

Barr, James. "Theophany and Anthropomorphism in the Old Testament." *Supplements to Vetus Testamentum*. Leiden: E. J. Brill, 1960.

Barrett, Justin L., and Frank C. Keil. "Conceptualizing a Nonnatural Entity: Anthropomorphism in God Concepts." *Cognitive Psychology* 31 (1996) 219–47.

Blumenthal, David. "Tselem: Toward an Anthropopathic Theology of Image." http://www.js.emory.edu/BLUMENTHAL/image2.html.

Boesel, Chris, and Catherine Keller, editors. *Apophatic Bodies: Negative Theology, Incarnation, and Relationality*. New York: Fordham University Press, 2010.

Boyarin, Daniel. *The Jewish Gospels: The Story of the Jewish Christ*. New York: New Press, 2012.

Bucur, Bogdan G. "Exegesis of Biblical Theophanies in Byzantine Hymnography: Rewritten Bible?" *Theological Studies* 68 (2007) 92–112.

Burnett, Joel. *Where Is God? Divine Absence in the Hebrew Bible*. Minneapolis: Fortress, 2010.

Coates, Ruth. "Bakhtin and Hesychasm." *Religion & Literature* 37.3 (2005) 59–80.

Dombrowski, Daniel A. "Does God Have a Body?" *The Journal of Speculative Philosophy* 2.3 (1988) 225–32.

Elshtain, Jean Bethke. *Augustine and the Limits of Politics*. Notre Dame: University of Notre Dame Press, 1995.

Epley, Nicholas, Adam Waytz, and John T. Cacioppo. "On Seeing Human: A Three-Factor Theory of Anthropomorphism." *Psychological Review* 114.4 (2007) 864–86.

———. "When We Need a Human: Motivational Determinants of Anthropomorphism." *Social Cognition* 26.2 (2008) 143–55.

FitzGerald, Thomas. "The Holy Eucharist as Theophany." *Greek Orthodox Theological Review* 28.1 (1983) 27–38.

Glock, Charles Y. "Images of God, Images of Man, and the Organization of Social Life." *Journal for the Scientific Study of Religion* 11.1 (1972) 1–15.

Guthrie, Stewart Elliott. *Faces in the Clouds: a New Theory of Religion*. New York: Oxford University Press, 1993.

Hamori, Esther J. *When Gods Were Men: the Embodied God in Biblical and Near Eastern Literature*. New York: Walter De Gruyter, 2008.

Heijne, Camilla Helena von. *The Messenger of the Lord in Early Jewish Interpretations of Genesis*. New York: Walter De Gruyter, 2010.

Hengel, Martin. *The Son of God: The Origin of Christology and the History of Jewish-Hellenistic Religion*. 1976. Reprint, Eugene, OR: Wipf & Stock, 1976.

Hill, Peter C., and Todd W. Hall. "Relational Schemas in Processing One's Image of God and Self." *Journal of Psychology and Christianity* 21.4 (2002) 1–28.

Hunt, W. Murray. "Some Remarks about the Embodiment of God." *Religious Studies* 17.1 (1981) 105–8.

Jones, John D. "Filled with the Visible Theophany of the Lord: Reading Dionysius East and West." Unpublished Lecture. Duquesne University, September 2010.

Kennedy, J. S. *The New Anthropomorphism.* New York: Cambridge University Press, 1992.

Lossky, Vladimir. *In the Image and Likeness of God.* Edited by John H. Erickson and Thomas E. Bird. Crestwood: St. Vladimir's Seminary Press, 1974.

McFague, Sallie. "The World as God's Body." *Religion Online.* http://www.religion-online. org/showarticle.asp?title=56.

Meier, Brian P., et al. "What's 'Up' With God? Vertical Space as a Representation of the Divine." *Journal of Personality and Social Psychology* 93.5 (2007) 699–710.

Miller, David L. *Three Faces of God: Traces of the Trinity in Literature and Life.* Philadelphia: Fortress, 1986.

Nauert, Nick. "Why Do We Anthropomorphize?" *PsychCentral.* http://psychcentral.com/ news/2010/03/01/why-do-we-anthropomorphize/11766.html.

Nes, Solrunn. *The Uncreated Light. An Iconographical Study of the Transfiguration in the Eastern Church.* Translated by Arlyne Moi. Grand Rapids: Eerdmans Publishing Company, 2007.

Neusner, Jacob. *The Incarnation of God: the Character of Divinity in Formative Judaism.* Philadelphia: Fortress, 1988.

Nicholas of Cusa. *The Vision of God.* Translated by E. G. Salter. New York: Ungar, 1969.

Niebuhr, Reinhold. *Moral Man and Immoral Society: A Study in Ethics and Politics.* New York: Scribner's, 1934.

Nikkel, David H. *Radical Embodiment.* Eugene, OR: Pickwick, 2010.

O'Neill, John. *Five Bodies: Re-figuring Relationships.* Thousand Oaks, CA: SAGE, 2004.

Orlov, Andrei. "Praxis of the Voice: The Divine Name Traditions in the Apocalypse of Abraham." *Journal of Biblical Literature* 127.1 (2008) 53–70.

———. and Alexander Golitzin. "'Many Lamps are Lightened from the One.' Paradigms of the Transformational Vision in Macarian Homilies." http://www.marquette.edu/ maqom/hesychasm.html.

Pelikan, Jaroslav. *The Christian Tradition. A History of the Development of Doctrine. Volume 2, the Spirit of eastern Christiandom (600–1700).* Chicago: University of Chicago Press, 1974.

Pollner, Melvin. "Divine Relations, Social Relations, and Well-Being." *Journal of Health and Social Behavior* 30.1 (1989) 92–104.

Reich, K. Helmut. "The Person–God Relationship: A Dynamic Model." *The International Journal for the Psychology of Religion* 13.4 (2003) 229–47.

Shepherd, Massey Hamilton, Jr. "The Anthropomorphic Controversy in the Time of Theophilus of Alexandria." *Church History* 7.3 (1938) 263–73.

Sommer, Benjamin. *The Bodies of God and the World of Ancient Israel.* Cambridge: Cambridge University Press, 2009.

St. Augustine. *Confessions, Book IV.* http://sparks.eserver.org/books/augustineconfess. pdf.

St. Clair, Michael. *Human Relationships and the Experience of God.* New York: Paulist Press, 1994.

Church Bodies

St. Irenaeus of Lyons. *On the Apostolic Teaching*. Crestwood, NY: St. Vladimir's Seminary Press, 1997.

St. John of Damascus. *On the Divine Images: Three Apologies Against Those Who Attack the Divine Images*. Translated by David Anderson. Crestwood, NY: St. Vladimir's Seminary Press, 1980.

Terrien, Samuel. *The Elusive Presence: Towards a New Biblical Theology*. San Francisco: Harper & Row, 1978.

Tracy, Thomas F. *God, Action, and Embodiment*. Grand Rapids: Eerdmans, 1984.

Wainwright, William J. "God's Body." *Journal of the American Academy of Religion* 42.3 (1974) 470–81.

Williams, Wesley. "Sapphiric God: Esoteric Speculation of the Body Divine in Biblical and Post–Biblical Jewish Tradition: Part I." http://drwesleywilliams.com/yahoo_site_admin/assets/docs/Sapphiric_Part_I.471537.pdf.

CHAPTER 6

On Becoming What We Are

A Hegelian Interpretation of Eucharistic Embodiment

John M. Bechtold

IT SHOULD COME AS no surprise that, in both the history of Western philosophy and of Christian theology, the body is often neglected, overlooked, or outright condemned. This is particularly odd for Christian theology given that its distinction and uniqueness stems from the doctrine of the incarnation. The church often claims, "God is like Jesus," (which, of course, in no way discounts the claim that "Jesus is God"), but the Jesus that is spoken of is often superhuman (in fairly obvious ways), or inhuman insofar as he often lacks genuine relationships, emotions, and natural processes. The obvious trouble with a superhuman or inhuman Jesus is that the distinctiveness of the Christian faith is utterly lost. Instead of claiming, "God is like Jesus," the claim merely becomes, "Jesus is like God," which greatly diminishes the import of the Christ-event in the world. Just as problematic as the doctrinal aspect, such theology also heavily influences the actual bodies of those who so think. A superhuman/inhuman Jesus often leads to a potentially dangerous focus on orthodoxy as entirely distinct from ethical and moral considerations. A dehumanized Christianity is not really Christianity at all.

The disembodiment of Christianity, which is an ultimate cause of its dehumanization, has strong resonance, and certainly some form of cause and effect relation to, a similar disembodiment found in Western philosophy. Philosophers like Martin Heidegger, of course, would lay blame for this phenomenon at the feet of Plato,[1] but it's certainly the case that Plato was not the first nor the only great thinker to envision a strong dualism of mind and body. Although space constraints preclude a full genealogical examination of philosophical rejection of the body, a brief overview will be helpful in pointing out the ethical shortcomings of such a position. These ethical shortcomings should be a primary catalyst, although by no means the catalyst, for a re-invigorated philosophical exploration of the body.

Within the Christian tradition, one of the most obvious ways that the body is neglected, if not implicitly rejected, is in the common notion that Christianity at least begins with, and perhaps is entirely determined by, one's mental assent to one or more propositions. This understanding of Christianity tends to reject many historical Christian practices in favor of cognitive emotionalism and ethical emotivism. One strong example can be seen in the 19th Century American Holiness movement from which many contemporary Arminian-Wesleyan denominations have sprung. Charles Edwin Jones describes this situation well. "Holiness believers generally approved of contemporary social standards and identified current taboos with the sins of the Spirit . . . evangelistic workers instructed seekers after perfect love to forsake inward sins (pride, covetousness, etc.) by adopting standards already approved by the sanctified."[2]

The American Holiness movement was strongly influenced by the theology of John Wesley and of early Methodism. In particular, one can point to Wesley's definition of sin "properly so-called," as an early example of, and a foundational undergirding for, the potential disembodiment of Holiness theology and ethics. Importantly and controversially, Wesley took the notion of sin outside of direct bodily actions into the realm of intentionality. An action itself is never sinful unless it is motivated by a negative will. Wesley claimed that sin is "a voluntary transgression of a known law

---

1. E.g. "The fact that Plato did not advance far enough so as ultimately to see beings themselves and in a certain sense to overcome dialectic is a deficiency included in his own dialectical procedure, and it determines certain moments in his dialectic. . .These characteristics are not merits and are not determinations of a superior philosophical method but are indications of a fundamental confusion and unclarity." Heidegger, *Plato's Sophist*, 137. Given the nature of this essay, it is interesting to note that Heidegger blames both Plato and dialectic for this problem. This essay will argue in greater detail that dialectical thought, at least as conceived by Hegel, offers the possibility of a profound philosophy of embodiment.

2. Jones, *Perfectionist Persuasion, 1867–1936*, 6.

[of God]."[3] The difficulty arises in that Wesley was careful not to allow his hamartiology to be entirely volitional. Individuals are still responsible for what Wesley termed "sin improperly so called," which is "an involuntary transgression of a divine law, known or unknown."[4] Such a transgression still "needs the atoning blood, and without this would expose to eternal damnation."[5] Although it seems questionable whether distinguishing between sins "properly" and "improperly" so called is a meaningful philosophical endeavor, Wesley maintained that, what he meant by Christian perfection, would in no way abolish sins "improperly so called." Wesley deemed this continuing failure as "naturally consequent on the ignorance and mistakes inseparable from *mortality*."[6]

While Wesley clearly did not have a high view of human nature, the fact remains that the particular actions of a human body, regardless of intentionality, had soteriological ramifications. Moving beyond Wesley, however, many "Holiness" Christians went on to claim that a person ceased to sin upon being entirely sanctified. The obvious problem with this claim is that it allowed such sanctified Christians to live without intentionally considering their bodily actions. Righteousness was presupposed, not enacted. One of the most damning examples of this presupposed righteousness is seen in the splitting of the Methodist Episcopal Church. While this split was ostensibly caused by regional opinions about slavery, the immorality of slavery was often left unquestioned, even by those in the North. The Northern Methodists continued to incorporate slave-holding border conferences within their ranks. Many so-called "perfectionists" were involved in these conferences, which "showed them to be more interested in sectional dominance than in racial justice."[7] While this is only a singular example, even if

3. Wesley, *Thoughts on Christian Perfection*, q.6 ans.1, cited in Albert Outler, *John Wesley*, 287.

4. Ibid.

5. Ibid.

6. Ibid., q.1 ans.3, 287. It is interesting to note that, even while speaking of a person as mortal, Wesley seems to do so in a way that ignores actual bodily actions. The body is weak, and therefore not responsible for its shortcomings. Here, at least, Wesley clearly treats the body as distinct from the person. By demarcating between bodily actions and the ethical person, Wesley conceives of a disembodied Christianity that is judged solely by what it believes to be the case, rather than by the way it interacts within the world. While this was certainly not Wesley's intention, insofar as he placed great value on particular bodily actions, this is certainly a logical direction for those who follow Wesley's thought.

7. Jones, *Perfectionist Persuasion*, 9.

a strong one, of the moral shortcomings made possible by a disembodied Christianity, it is in no way unique. Countless examples could be given of bodily ethical failings occurring under the guise of Christian moral purity. Wesley's emphasis on sins of intention made this prevalent within Wesleyan/Holiness ranks. As such, it is becoming more and more important to reject a Christian philosophy of sin that has at its core intention removed from action. The Christian mind can no longer take precedence over the Christian body.

In order to regain an important focus on the body, this essay will move forward in what might seem to be a strange place: the philosophy of G.W.F. Hegel. Hegel, of course, is often caricatured as the great Spiritualist, as an absolute idealist, and as the last great practitioner of pure dualism. Readers of Hegel often begin with the assumption that Hegel's system represents the forward-moving march of *Geist* across history. Hegel, it is argued, cannot escape the critique that all change is progress, that all movement is good movement. These caricatures of Hegel tend to be neither accurate nor helpful. Such critiques of Hegel fail to recognize the essential notion in Hegel's thought that *Geist* itself does not actually move through history. History is made by people, while *Geist* merely explicates itself through this historical march of those people. Hegel, therefore, actually has much to offer to a discussion of embodiment.

The point of this essay is not merely to explicate Hegel, of course, but to utilize Hegelian thought in service to the Christian church, particularly in overcoming the sort of disembodied Christianity that has been described previously. While there are many ways to approach the concept of embodiment from within the Christian tradition, one of the easiest ways to do so will be through a discussion of the sacraments. Eucharist, in particular, involves a multi-faceted embodiment. Eucharist takes seriously Jesus' own subjective embodiment, that is, the historical reality of Jesus›s physical form. Likewise, Eucharist as a practice necessarily requires the physical bodies of its participants. On a third level, Eucharist also involves a literal in-bodiment, the physical consumption of an actual morsel of food and drink. At the heart of eucharistic practice is the proclamation regarding the bread, "This is the body of Christ, broken for you." Eucharist, as sacrament, is a means of grace. This grace, of which Eucharist is the means, is itself bodily and embodied.

Hegel offers an important means by which to describe the embodiment of grace that takes place in sacramental practice. Hegel is misunderstood if one claims that the explication of Geist throughout history is a pre-ordained, or purely positive/progressive, happening. To make this claim requires a misrepresentation of dialectics. Dialectics is not a process of consensus but of negativity. There is no "synthesis" in Hegel's dialectics. Rather, Hegel describes a process by which any proposition, if understood linguistically, or any subject, if understood metaphysically, already contains within itself its own negation. Eucharist, likewise, is a profoundly negative moment: broken body, shed blood, etc. Yet, Hegel would take it one step farther by claiming that Eucharist is also a negativizing moment. The grace of which Eucharist is a means is already present in the body of the participant. Particularly within a Wesleyan context, this extant grace is descriptively called prevenient insofar as it is always already present. Going back to Hegel's language, this prevenient grace is the determinate negation of the subject, which is enacted via Eucharistic practice. By physically embodying the claim, «This is the body of Christ,» the participant embraces the negativizing effects of the grace which was always already present.

In a very important, and surprisingly lucid, section of *Science of Logic*[8] Hegel gives an account of the dialectical system that undergirds so much of his thought. This accounting of dialectic, in particular, goes a long way to dispel the simplistic, and frankly wrong, description of dialectic that is often seen in introductory philosophical textbooks and classes. Rather than speaking in terms of thesis-antithesis-synthesis, which is a triad that Hegel never applies directly to his own thought, he speaks of dialectic as a threefold movement of Being-Nothing-Becoming. Hegel describes Being as such: "In its indeterminate immediacy it is equal only to itself . . . It has no diversity within itself, nor any with a reference outward . . . There is *nothing* to be intuited in it . . . Being, the indeterminate immediate, is in fact *nothing*, and neither more nor less than *nothing*."[9] Hegel makes it very clear, here, that the first and second movements of dialectic, Being and Nothing, are actually much more closely related than they are complete opposites. The second movement of dialectic is not "antithesis." The second movement is, in some form, an overcoming, but it is not a simple reversal.

Hegel describes this second movement, Nothing, in this way: "Nothing, pure nothing . . . is simply equality with itself, complex emptiness, absence of all determination and content—undifferentiatedness in itself."[10]

8. Hegel, *Science of Logic*.

9. Ibid., 82.

10. Ibid.

At face value, this brief description of Nothing sounds very similar to the previous description of Being. Hegel continues, "In so far as intuiting or thinking can be mentioned here, it counts as a distinction whether something or *nothing* is intuited or thought. To intuit or think nothing has, therefore, a meaning; both are distinguished and thus *nothing* is (exists) in our intuiting or thinking. Nothing is, therefore, the same determination, or rather absence of determination, and thus altogether the same as, pure *being*."[11] Of course, it should be no surprise that when Hegel says that Nothing is "altogether the same as" Being, this does not mean that there is no distinction or differentiation between the terms. According to Hegel, "It is equally true that they are not undistinguished from each other, that, on the contrary, they are not the same, that they are absolutely distinct, and yet that they are unseparated and inseparable."[12]

Even so, despite the complexity with which Hegel writes, there is still an important element to his thought, here, that ought not to be too quickly passed over. The key to understanding Hegel's thought is that there is no synthesis of Being and Nothing. The dialectical movement does not seek synthesis, and, indeed, could never achieve synthesis anyway. The fact that the first two dialectical movements Being and Nothing are distinct yet inseparable, is evidence that the Hegelian system should not be considered a purely positive and progressive forward-marching movement. Even in those times when Hegel speaks of the progression of history in such a way, it is only from the present, looking backward, that such a claim could be made. Hegel may make claims to the superiority of certain ideas over others, or of course of certain religions, peoples, etc., but in a profoundly important way, even those ideas which he sees as superior, are themselves inextricably tied to those which are 'inferior.' Speaking of Being and Nothing, Hegel said, "Their truth is, therefore, this movement of the immediate vanishing of the one in the other: *becoming*, a movement in which both are distinguished, but by a difference which has equally immediately resolved itself."[13]

The first movement of dialectic is not merely overcome by its direct opposite, but is transformed by a difference which was always already present even in the initial movement itself. A thesis is not transformed by means of its antithesis, but by an internal and pre-existent Nothing. This Nothing

11. Ibid.

12. Ibid., 83.

13. Ibid.

is not a particular Nothing, which relates directly to a specific 'something.' Rather, "Nothing is to be taken in its indeterminate simplicity."[14] By way of example, most people have probably heard this or a similar argument being made: atheism, as such, is a problematic concept because the claim, "I do not believe in God," always leaves open the claim, "Which God do you not believe in?" This kind of apologetics is not at all what Hegel has in mind. The Nothing which transforms Being is not open to the question, "Which nothing?" It is not the nothing of a particular something. Nothing, that is, is not merely the opposite of any particular form of Being. According to Hegel, "We are concerned first of all not with the form of opposition (with the form, that is, also of relation) but with the abstract, immediate negation: nothing, purely on its own account, negation devoid of any relations—what could also be expressed if one so wished merely by (the word) 'not.'"[15] A particular Nothing which is the inversion of a particular "something" is not what Hegel is after here. Yet, he also sees that both Being and Nothing are but moments of Becoming insofar as their present and continuous movement is to vanish into one another. Becoming, then, as the third dialectical movement is not merely the unity of Being and Nothing, and certainly not if these are abstracted from themselves. Much less is Becoming a synthesis of the two. To the contrary, Becoming is "the determinate unity in which there is both being and nothing."[16] Both exist "in this unity, but only as vanishing, sublated moments."[17] Insofar as both are vanishing sublated moments, both Being and Nothing are themselves unities of being and nothing. "The one is being as immediate and as relation to nothing, and the other is nothing as immediate and as relation to being."[18] Both Being and Nothing differ in focus, and in direction, but, "both are the same, *becoming*, and although they differ so in direction, they interpenetrate and paralyze each other."[19] Both Being and Nothing are part and parcel of Becoming. Yet, it is also true that the relationship between Being and Nothing is not one of reciprocity. It is not only that Being and Nothing as external movements come together in a process of Becoming. "The one does not sublate the other externally—but each sublates itself in itself and is in its

14. Ibid.
15. Ibid.
16. Ibid., 103.
17. Ibid., 105.
18. Ibid.
19. Ibid.

own self the opposite of itself."[20] The process of becoming, this internal self-sublation of Being and Nothing, is not mere transitoriness, but in some sense settles into a stable unity of change. Although he was not directly referring to Hegel, and would certainly be uncomfortable with the analogy, this idea is very similar to Gilles Deleuze's concept of "chaosmos."[21] To use the term 'chaosmos' in this manner would be to demonstrate that change itself, becoming in motion, is not a particular event, but the status quo by which all things move. Deleuzian 'chaosmos,' and Hegelian Becoming, do not exist as synthetic, but are embodied in flux. Like the actual occasions of process philosophy, Becoming can be viewed as intrinsically distinct, but only insofar as it is always already negating and re-envisioning itself.

Perhaps it would be helpful to transition back to a more direct discussion of bodies in order not to perpetuate the stereotype that says that Hegel has nothing to say to the real world. Indeed, it also deserves mentioning that several hundred pages of *Science of Logic*, a text which most casual readers of Hegel avoid, are dedicated to issues of physics, mechanics, and chemistry. However, this essay is not intended to be a discursis on these particular matters. Rather, the intention here is to offer a way by which Hegel's systematic philosophy could serve as a reasonable grounding for Christian theological discussion. Hegel has a great deal to say about the development of human persons, and he recognizes that any discussion of human development simultaneously requires an explanation of bodies. Within the Christian theological context, one likewise cannot simply begin with the practice of Eucharist, or even of Passover, but must begin with the notion of the universe, and its inhabitants as creation.

Given the constraints of space it would be easiest to skip over the idea of an actual punctiliar beginning, a notion which Hegel has great difficulty

20. Ibid., 106.

21. While Deleuze would balk at the suggestion, a strong argument could be made that Deleuze was entirely more reliant on Hegel than he realized. He repeatedly uses the term 'chaosmos,' sometimes with reference to James Joyce, other times with reference to Lewis Carroll, and yet other times without literary reference, to make a profoundly Hegelian point. E.g., "Ontology is the dice throw, the chaosmos from which the cosmos emerges. If the imperatives of Being have a relation with the I, it is with the fractured I in which, every time, they displace and reconstitute the fracture according to the order of time." Deleuze, *Difference and Repetition*, 199. Or, elsewhere, Deleuze uses verse to describe chaosmos evolutionarily, "Between night and day, between that which is constructed and that which grows naturally, between mutations from the inorganic to the organic, from plant to animal, from animal to humankind, yet without this series constituting a progression." Deleuze and Guattari, *Thousand Plateaus*, 313.

with, and simply recognize existence.[22] Hegel's most well-known book is, after all, a phenomenology, and in that work he speaks of "the element of immediate existence" as the beginning of Science, which is to say, of systematic philosophy.[23] Taking what has been explored in the preceding discussion, it is not difficult to transpose the concept of embodied human development into Hegel's notion of dialectic. Such a move is well warranted by Hegel who believed that any proper philosophy needed to be "scientific." By this he meant that the point of philosophy was to create, or discover, a system by which all things could be explained. Hegel would not have conceded that a philosopher might need different systems to fit different contexts. Rather, he claimed that a single system, which he, of course, believed himself to have discovered, could be the end of philosophy insofar as it would serve as an outline for all understanding. Thus, Hegel used his system to discuss aesthetics, world history, religion, anthropology, etc. To transpose the dialectic onto embodied human development is a very Hegelian move.

Presupposing physical existence, the question is how best to insert human beings into the dialectic. Hegel argued against a strong dualism, which was and is rampant in Christian thought, by using the term 'spirit' to describe a holistic idea. Humans, for Hegel, are spiritual. To say that humans are spiritual is not to argue that a person's essence is to be found in a transcendent soul, but rather that both body and soul, an inseparable combination, are better spoken of as forces than as things. Hegel says, "Spirit is not that contradiction which the things is, which dissolves itself . . . on the contrary, it is already in its own self the contradiction that has returned into its absolute unity . . . in which the differences are no longer to be thought of as independent, but only as particular, moments in the subject, in the simple individuality."[24] When Hegel speaks of humans as spiritual beings, he clearly is not operating within a strongly dualistic framework. Of course, it is not only with direct reference to humanity that Hegel speaks of Spirit. Hegel also speaks at great length of Spirit with a capital 's,' which, for the sake of differentiation from human spirit will here be referred to as *Geist*.

22. Hegel's difficulty with a punctiliar beginning, and likewise his difficulty with a punctiliar ending, lies in the nature of processive becoming. Hegel describes Being as only meaningful in relation to Nothing, as itself already negative. If the world exists only as Becoming, Hegel struggles to find a way to articulate a definitive point that would lie outside, either at the beginning or the end, of this process.

23. Hegel, *Phenomenology of Spirit*, §35.

24. Hegel, *Science of Logic*, 498.

Yet, as with human spirit, *Geist* is not ethereal, disembodied, or entirely transcendent.

Geist is, of course, transcendent, but in Hegel's description of the term, transcendent is not necessarily distinct from embodiment. Consider, for example, what might be called "school spirit." Walking around any particular campus one will encounter t-shirts, posters, sweats, and coffee mugs that are all emblazoned with the requisite school logo. Most colleges have athletic team, and the games played by these teams are, one would hope, attended by many students. The students watching these games cheer for on their classmates often using terms like "us," "we," and "our" to place themselves within the athletic team itself. "We've got this," those students might proclaim. "Nobody can touch our defense tonight." These students, as well as faculty, staff, and alumni, support their school's athletic teams and fine arts programs, and give of their time and money to the benefit of the school. The reason for all of these things could be described as "school spirit." School spirit exists in a real and profound way in the embodied actions of these supporters. Yet, whatever it is that is meant by "school spirit," while entirely reliant on embodied actions, is also transcendent to those actions. It exists as an efficacious idea, a movement, perhaps even a longing. In the same way, Hegel's understanding of *Geist* is both embodied and transcendent. It is not defined solely by embodied actions, but its existence is entirely reliant upon them. "The True is the whole. But the whole is nothing other than the essence consummating itself through its development. Of the Absolute it must be said that it is essentially a *result*, that only in the *end* is it what it truly is; and that precisely in this consists its nature, viz. to be actual, subject the spontaneous becoming of itself."[25]

Humanity is an objective and determinate form for *Geist* and is, therefore, both Being and Nothing. Such an Hegelian understanding of spiritual embodiment offers a particularly interesting commentary on eucharistic practice. If true Becoming is the simultaneous interpenetration of both Being and Nothing then one could argue that creation, as a living and developing concept, itself a Becoming, is also both Being and Nothing. Such a concept calls into question a fairly common Christian assumption that the early stories of Genesis represent a discussion about The Fall of humankind. That is, it is presumed, with some textual warrant, that something fundamentally changed in the world as the forbidden fruit crossed Eve's lips (and perhaps those of Adam as well). Given a literal historical reading,

25. Hegel, *Phenomenology of Spirit*, §20.

this is a fair interpretation of the biblical text. However, an alternative interpretation, also with textual warrant, would claim that sin and brokenness did not instantaneously appear because of the single act of a single individual. Rather, both of the Genesis creation stories describe a creation that is already broken. God's declaration that it is "good" is not proof of a primordial perfection, but the recognition that even the brokenness of the world, whether actual or potential, is, itself, natural. This is not, however, God's invitation to "sin boldly."

Genesis's first story of creation presumes that the act of creation is a superficial structuring imposed on a primordial chaos. This structuring is not absolute, and, as the story of the Flood makes clear, is only maintained by God's continuous hand. What Hegel calls Nothing, is therefore constantly in flux with the Being of creation. Genesis's second creation story further describes this reality in God's realization that it is not good for a person to be alone. Here, in the midst of the initial creative activity, it would appear, loneliness, or what might be called psychological nothingness is already present. Adam, the prototypical person exists as Being and Nothing. Adam, in that sense, is not created as fully formed but as a "becoming-person." Creation, as both Being and Nothing is continually creative and continually created. Creation is not static but in-process.

It is, within the Christian tradition, grace which moves creation toward redemption. The created world is inherently gracious. This is the point at which Eucharist, as sacrament, can again be considered. Eucharist is not a practice of redemption imposed from without, but a practice of becoming what we already are. John Wesley recognized this in his sermon, "The Duty of Constant Communion." Wesley said, "The grace of God given herein confirms to us the pardon of our sins, by enabling us to leave them."[26] Wesley is clear that the function of Eucharistic grace is to strengthen that grace which is already present in the participant. "As our bodies are strengthened by bread and wine, so are our souls by these tokens of the body and blood of Christ."[27] Augustine, likewise, recognized this aspect of already-present grace in Eucharistic practice. With regard to the Eucharist, Augustine said, "Be what you can see, and receive what you are."[28] For Augustine, as for Wesley, Eucharist makes manifest prevenient grace. This is precisely the de-

26. Wesley, "Sermon 101: The Duty of Constant Communion."

27. Ibid.

28. Augustine, "Sermon 272: On the Day of Pentecost to the *Infantes*, On the Sacrament," 298.

velopmental understanding proposed by Hegel. Novelty arises not from the blue but from the existent. Becoming is an evolutionary process wherein Being and Nothing are held in tension. Neither Being nor Nothing fully counteracts the other, but both, in their mutual interpenetration, purify each other. Redemption, in this sense, is both Being and Nothing. Eucharist, likewise, is the Becoming of redemption.

The "nothingness" of Eucharistic grace is death which is itself life. Hegel's teleology contains profoundly Aristotelian moments. The acorn must be sublated by the oak tree that is always already inherent therein. Likewise, the negation of the Eucharist is the negation of an 'I' which exists *für sich*. This "I" represents the pure Being of the first stage of dialectic. Yet, also present is an "I" which exists *an sich*, which is the Nothing of the second stage of dialectic. Hegel recognizes in this bifurcated "I" developmental possibilities. "In order to comprehend what development is—what may be called two different states must be distinguished. The first is what is known as capacity, power, what I call being-in-itself (*potential, dunamis*); the second principle is that of being-for-itself, actuality (*actus, energeia*)."[29] This being-in-itself, the potential for something more, exists as Nothing, ready to sublate the actuality of Being. Thus, for Hegel, the process of development is one of becoming what one already is. *Potentia* is never extrinsic, even to the Being *für sich*. "If we say, for example, that man is by nature rational, we would mean that he has reason only inherently or in embryo . . . But while the child only has capacities or the actual possibility of reason, it is just the same as if he had no reason; reason does not yet exist in him since he cannot yet do anything rational, and has no rational consciousness. Thus what man is at first implicitly becomes explicit."[30]

Moving beyond Hegel's direct language, a Christian philosopher could very easily read "redemption" in place of Hegel's "reason." Creation, as described in Genesis, exists both *an sich* and *für sich*. As actual, even from the outset, creation exists as already broken. Yet inherent in creation is the potential for redemption. Creation, in the beginning, is already redeemed, but must become what it already is. For the Christian church, the sacraments exist as the means of grace by which this transformation happens. Eucharist presupposes its end, redemption, as its beginning. Redemption, however, as both the beginning and end of creation, only becomes actual

29. Hegel, *Lectures on the History of Philosophy Vol. I: Greek Philosophy to Plato*, 20–21.

30. Ibid., 21.

through ritual enactment. Redemption, then, is always embodied, always practiced. Eucharist is not a mere remembrance of the incarnation, but, as a means of grace, is the embodiment of incarnate life through the nothingness of death. At the Eucharistic table, participants become what they already are: redeemed. The practice of Eucharist becomes what Hegel calls that "being or immediacy whose mediation (redemption) is not outside it, but which is this mediation (redemption) itself."[31] In Eucharistic embodiment, redemption becomes manifest by "looking the negative in the face, and tarrying with it."[32]

---

31. Hegel, *Phenomenology of Spirit*, 19.
32. Ibid.

BIBLIOGRAPHY

Augustine. "Sermon 272: On the Day of Pentecost to the *Infantes*, On the Sacrament." In *The Works of Saint Augustine III/7*, edited by John E. Rotelle. Hyde Park, NY: New City, 1993.

Deleuze, Gilles. *Difference and Repetition*. Translated by Paul Patton. New York: Columbia Press, 2004.

Delueze, Gilles, and Felix Guattari. *A Thousand Plateaus: Capitalism and Schizophrenia*, tr. Brian Massumi. Minneapolis: University of Minnesota Press, 2003.

Hegel, G. W. F. *Lectures on the History of Philosophy, Vol. I: Greek Philosophy to Plato*. Translated by E. S. Haldane. Lincoln: University of Nebraska Press, 1995.

―――. *Phenomenology of Spirit*. Translated by A. V. Miller. New York: Oxford University Press, 1977.

―――. *Science of Logic*. Translated by A. V. Miller. Amherst, NY: Humanity, 1998.

Heidegger, Martin. *Plato's Sophist*. Translated by Richard Rojcewicz and André Schuwer. Bloomington: Indiana University Press, 2003.

Jones, Charles Edwin. *Perfectionist Persuasion: The Holiness Movement and American Methodism, 1867–1936*. Lanham: Scarecrow, 2002.

Outler, Albert. *John Wesley*. New York: Oxford University Press, 1964.

Altered Bodies

CHAPTER 7

Fracturing

The Eucharist, Body Modification,
and the Aesthetics of Brokenness

Brannon Hancock

WHEN I WAS AN undergraduate at a Christian liberal-arts university in Nashville, Tennessee, I became close friends with a young man who did not look like the typical student at our small, sheltered school. He had a shaved head, extensive tattooing and ear piercings that he was in the process of stretching or "gauging" out into larger holes. While he was certainly not the first person I'd met with tattoos or body piercings, he was the first person I ever heard use the phrase *body modification*, and so I became aware of an entire subculture of modified individuals who share in common the celebration of the manipulation, marking and gradual transformation of their bodies, not simply for decorative or traditionally fashionable purposes, but rather as part of life-long and often very spiritually-driven "body projects" which seek to remake the body according to some self-conceived vision and which intend to subvert the body and mark it as irrevocably "outside" mainstream culture.

In the intervening time, my own academic pursuits have taken me into the area of sacramental and liturgical theology, but as I have sought to deal with questions of culture and correlation as a student in a center for interdisciplinary theology, my mind has continually been drawn back to the subject of the modified body because of the way the practices undertaken by the subculture, or, more accurately, the overlapping subcultures, discussed in this paper resonate with certain metaphors and motifs that are operable within, and are even constitutive of, Christian sacramental theology, namely, that of the Eucharist. I want to examine what I call an "aesthetics of brokenness" in the secular rituals of the body modification subculture and in Christian Eucharistic practice.

DEFINING THE TERMS

Mike Featherstone defines *body modification* thusly:

> The term 'body modification' refers to a long list of practices which include piercing, tattooing, branding, cutting, binding and inserting implants to alter the appearance and form of the body. The list of these practices could be extended to include gymnastics, bodybuilding, anorexia and fasting—forms in which the body surface is not directly inscribed . . .[1]

In a more recent work, Victoria Pitts distinguishes between subversive or non-mainstream body mods and those that are more normative, or at least acceptable, in contemporary culture, and for my purposes, I wish to follow her distinction. Indeed, body modification, construed as loosely as possible, could include cultural practices ranging from the cosmetic (e.g. diet regimes, body building, plastic surgery, even spa practices) and even to medical or technological modifications (e.g. eyeglasses, prostheses, pacemakers, organ transplants; transgender / gender reassignment could be considered here as well) as well as the unapologetically counter-cultural mods (e.g. tattooing, scarification, piercing, branding, sub- and trans-dermal implants) that are the focus of this paper. Pitts writes:

> The body shrinks in size through some of these practices, is built and sculpted in other practices. It is painted, wrapped, oiled, stretched, cut, implanted, excavated, sectioned, measured, and otherwise transformed . . . the body ingests and absorbs synthetic and organic materials, and is reshaped by lasers, plastics and sutures.[2]

1. Featherstone, *Body Modification*, 1.
2. Pitts, *In The Flesh*, 30.

While mainstream modifications such as small, decorative tattoos or fashionable body piercings are increasingly common in contemporary culture, my interest is in body modification practices that, by intention and design, subvert traditional body aesthetics. Therefore, I exclude those modifications which are societally encouraged and in-line with standards of beauty imposed by market forces (i.e. advertising, fashion, media), such as cosmetic surgeries designed to make a normal, healthy body appear *more* healthful, attractive, etc.

During my research into this subject, it became increasingly difficult for me to draw a boundary around the subculture or community that I wanted to talk about. For example, a great deal of overlap exists between:

- Heavily tattooed and pierced persons, who might (or might not) identify themselves as punks, goths, or other subcultures characterized largely by a particular "style" (or perhaps "anti-style")[3]

- Underground BDSM (bondage, domination & sado-masochism) culture,

- Cyberpunks,[4] who desire a merger between the body and technology,

- Performance artists, such as Orlan and Stelarc, who work with the body, and

- Modern primitives, who subscribe to the philosophies and rituals of primitive or tribal cultures as a resistance to our fragmentary, hypertechnologized consumer culture.

A BRIEF HISTORY: FROM MODERN PRIMITIVES TO BME AND THE CHURCH OF BODY MODIFICATION

Modern primitivism is a complex subculture some of whose roots can be traced to the S/M and fetish underground of the 1970s and 80s. In Victoria Pitts' words, modern primitivism "links body modifications to

3. The tattoo has a vast and variegated history that has been discussed at length elsewhere, and so I will forgo specific discussion of tattooing at this time, as the tattoo is merely a player in the broader aesthetic under examination here. However, a specific focus on tattooing—for instance, the resonance between the stigmatizing effects of the tattoo and phenomenon of the stigmata—would be fertile ground for further exploration.

4. Inspired by the science fiction novels of William Gibson, especially *Neuromancer* and *Mona Lisa Overdrive*.

non-Western, spiritual, communal rituals."[5] In addition to various permanent or semi-permanent body modifications that are associated with modern primitivism, such as stretched piercings, scarifications, brandings, facial tattoos and genital modifications, modern primitives also engage in rituals of body manipulation or "body play," which are believed to find their origins in tribal rituals and so, despite their appropriation and adaptation by the technologized West, are considered a gateway to a more "pure" or spiritual, yet highly idealized, way of life long passed.[6]

The person who has contributed the most to defining this movement is Fakir Musafar, who coined the term *modern primitivism* in 1978, and who now at age 83 is *the* icon of modern primitivism.[7] He considers body play practices "worship through the body."[8] While Fakir's influence on contemporary piercing and body mod rituals cannot be underestimated, the rise in popular interest in body modification and modern primitivism, and increased participation in the subculture over the past two decades, is also a direct result of the book *Modern Primitives*, published in 1985 (eds. V. Vale and A. Juno). The book, inspired in large part by Fakir Musafar, is a collection of interviews, photographs and articles about radical body modifiers; the modern primitives showcased in the book "present indigenous practices as alternatives to Western culture, which is perceived as alienated

---

5. Pitts, *In The Flesh*, 8.

6. Of course many of these rituals are still practiced in contemporary tribal cultures in the developing world, and the subculture's relationship to the primitive cultures that they are so quick to romanticize is a problematic and incredibly naïve one. Some theorists argue that modern primitives—mostly young, white persons—are actually practicing a form of colonialism, as they adopt a "pick-and-choose" approach to suit their own needs and desires, borrowing certain rituals without appreciating the whole of such cultures—their philosophies, social hierarchies, government, religion, etc.—and largely without concern for authenticity.

7. Fakir, born in 1930 in Aberdeen, South Dakota, began experimenting with his body as a teenager. Inspired by *National Geographic* and compelled by forces that he only ever describes in spiritual terms, Fakir self-administered his first piercing in the 1940s, at a time when (according to him) virtually no one in the West had unconventional piercings—he suggests that, had anyone known, he would have likely been pathologized and institutionalized for what he was doing at this time—and in the 1960s, when he sought to have significant blackwork tattooing applied to his torso (back and front), he struggled for five years before finding a tattooist willing to undertake the project. See V. Vale and A. Juno, *Modern Primitives*, 6–36.

8. Featherstone, *Body Modification*, 16.

from the body's spiritual, sexual, and communal potential."[9] In the introduction to *Modern Primitives,* the editors write:

> What is implied by the revival of "modern primitive" activities is the desire for, and the dream of, a *more ideal society*. Amidst an almost universal feeling of powerlessness to "change the world," individuals are changing what they *do* have power over: *their own bodies.*[10]

Modern Primitives was crucial in laying out the philosophical and spiritual impetus for the movement; it was amazingly successful, considering its subversive subject matter, and has gone through numerous reprints since its initial publication.

The two final "events" in the body mod movement that should be highlighted are the creation of the website *BME*, or body modification e-zine, by Shannon Larratt in 1994, and the founding of the Church of Body Modification in 2000. Since its inception in 1994, *BME* has become *the* central feature of the subculture and is largely responsible for any sense of "community" that exists amongst body modifiers. Victoria Pitts writes: "[Larratt] describes the purpose of BME as building a community of body modifiers that may be geographically dispersed but share a common sense of alienation from mainstream society."[11] *BME* contains biographies of and interviews with high-profile body modifiers, such as Fakir Musafar, Frances Sand, Steve Haworth and Larratt himself, and provides a forum wherein participants can discuss their mods, post photo documentation of their various transformations, and share their thoughts, experiences, encouragement and support with and for one another. Naturally, *BME* has led to the creation of other websites that serve the subculture, such as *Modified Mind* and *suspension.org.*

The Church of Body Modification is a direct outgrowth of the *BME* community, and is now a legally recognized (albeit loosely formed) non-denominational, interfaith congregation in the USA. It accepts members (via an online application) and has ordained several ministers. Like every church, it even has a mission statement! While no religious or denominational affiliation is nullified by virtue of one's membership, neither is any particular faith commitment necessary to become a member of the Church of Body Modification, apart from the belief that "ancient and modern body

9. Pitts, *In The Flesh*, 8.

10. Vale and Juno, *Modern Primitives*, 4.

11. Pitts, *In The Flesh*, 167.

modification rites . . . are essential to [one's] spirituality," and that these rituals "strengthen the bond between mind, body and soul . . . [and] ensure that we live as spiritually complete and healthy individuals." The *COBM* statement of faith includes articles like "respect [for] our bodies" and "our right to explore our world, both physical and supernatural, through spiritual body modification."[12]

In a certain sense, this community consists of individuals who share in a common story.[13] Often this narrative usually revolves around:

- Feelings of *alienation*—that is, the alienation of the self from others and even the self from the self;

- Feelings of *marginalization* within society due to one's outward appearance (after, and even sometimes before, modification);

- Feelings of *disease* with(in) one's own skin, the only antidote for which turns out to be the (gradual) transformation of the body;

- Feelings of *powerlessness* as the body becomes colonized by market forces within late-capitalist society, as the body becomes less necessary due to mechanical and technical processes within industry.

A final category worthy of its own study, but which I will only mention briefly, is that of women who have been sexually abused or raped and who undertake what Victoria Pitts calls "women's reclaiming rituals" wherein modifications rituals (scars, brands, tattoos or piercings) enable a woman to reconnect with her body following some sort of trauma. Many women who have had such experiences testify to the psycho-spiritual power of these body rituals to help them heal and become whole after a seemingly irrevocable loss.[14]

---

12. This and the following quotes are from The Church of Body Modification's doctrinal statement, available on their website. See: http://www.uscobm.com.

13. DeMello, *Inscription*, 18. DeMello points out that communities of body modifiers are, to a certain degree, a function of *discourse* contained within magazines, books and internet websites, and the shared experience of modifiers when they congregate at conventions or in tattoo parlors and body modification studios.

14. Pitts, *In the Flesh*, 49–86.

EUCHARISTIC BODIES: THE AESTHETICS OF BROKENNESS

As they raise issues of embodiment, subjectivity, community, politics, spirituality, beauty, and textuality, to name but a few, I find the practices of extreme body modifiers fertile ground for theological reflection, but today I just want to look at one theme. I begin by suggesting that in both the Eucharistic community and the body modification subculture, the prioritization of the *broken body* coalesces into an aesthetic that inverts and subverts traditional, societally-conditioned notions of beauty and instead celebrates the beauty of bodies marked and manipulated by processes of (intentional) wounding and healing, bodies bloodied, in pain, suspended and otherwise modified from their "natural" condition. (With an imagination formed by Christian worship, doctrine and iconography, I cannot look at bodies such as these without thinking, for instance, of the abject body of Christ in Grunewald's *Isenheim Alterpiece*.)

In the Christian tradition, the Eucharistic elements—wine representing Christ's spilled blood and the bread representing Christ's broken body—are given for mankind's salvation. According to Gregory Dix's 1945 classic *The Shape of the Liturgy*, the eucharistic narrative follows a poetic four-fold shape: the offertory, the Eucharistic prayer of consecration, the fraction, and the distribution or communion meal.[15] Put succinctly, the elements are *offered* (or *taken* by the priest), *blessed*, *broken* and *given*. Simultaneously, the congregation, as Christ's Body, passes through these four stages: We offer to God, to borrow the words of the Scottish Episcopal liturgy with which I am most familiar, "these gifts [of bread and wine], and with them ourselves, a single, holy, living sacrifice;" our bodies are blessed in the epiclesis (i.e. "send your Holy Spirit upon us and upon these elements"); and finally "the bread," the body of Christ, which now also includes the bodies of those who comprise the Church, "is broken for the life of the world" to which the congregation responds "Lord, unite us in this sign," this sign of brokenness; and just as the fracture of the bread necessarily precedes the distribution, so must the congregation be broken that we might be given. Our wholeness, as liturgical subjects, is fractured. Our unity, as a Body, is fragmentary. We are one, and we are many. Our (w)holiness is ripped through, our holes are exposed. The openings, the gaps, the distance not only between each individual and every other, but even within our divided

15. Dix, *Liturgy*, 48.

Selves,[16] is acknowledged and *enacted* in the breaking of the bread. It is no longer a loss to be mourned or overcome, but a celebration of our true humanity, broken yet redeemed, in Christ's fractured Body. It is through this sacred communion that the Church is transformed into the Body of Christ, God's vehicle of redemption in the world—in St. Augustine's words, at the table, we receive *what we are.* This brokenness turns out to be but the necessary prelude to the communion meal, which since the first century has scandalized the Christian faith—the body and blood of our Lord is our literal and spiritual food, and in that transubstantial, transgressive, transignificant moment, we become the very the meal we share with Christ and with one another—the Kingdom has come, and it is among us.

The Eucharist demonstrates the body at the point of utter abasement, abjection, abandonment and absence, and renarrates this body as *most really* present precisely in this absence, this moment of extreme kenosis— "*he made himself nothing*" (Phil. 2:7). The Eucharistic body is a subversive, scandalous, transgressive body. Mike Featherstone states that "[o]ne of the most objectionable aspects of body modification, for the wider public, is not just the prospect of a different aesthetics which goes counter to the notion of natural and consumer culture bodies, but the pain and violation of the body associated with cutting."[17] However, in her book *The Suffering Self*, Judith Perkins reinforces my sentiments well, at least as it concerns Christian thought, writing:

> Traditionally . . . [b]ruises, wounds, broken bodies, provided unassailable, palpable evidence of realized power. But Christian discourse reverses this equation and thus redefines some of the most basic signifiers in any culture—the body, pain, and death.[18]

The bodily brokenness that is integral to Christian practice subverts and inverts traditional aesthetics. In a logic in which life comes through death, and self through loss of self, Christ's sacrificial body, from the manger to the wilderness to the transfiguration to its suspension on the cross, and even in its resurrected form, vanishing at the table at Emmaus, still bearing the marks of the cross in the upper room . . . *This* body emerges as an image of profound beauty. Christ's wounds serve as the "opening" of the possibility

16. See Ricoeur, *Oneself as Another*, 1.

17. Featherstone, *Body Modification*, 8.

18. Perkins, *Suffering Self*, 115.

of humanity's communion with God. Wholeness is found in brokenness; the wound itself heals.

FIRST CRITIQUE: WHAT DOES THE EUCHARIST HAVE TO SAY ABOUT BODY MODIFICATION?

I want to briefly suggest that body mod practices resonate with Dix's four-fold shape in illuminating ways. Body modifiers offer their bodies, their very flesh and blood, to be altered, consecrated and finally broken, by the high priests of the subculture, namely, the artists and piercers. The breaking of the body is the central, redemptive, sacramental act. But it seems to me that the analogy breaks down at the fourth stage. While the brokenness of the modified body resonates with Eucharistic symbolism, and while body modifiers often emphasize an element of spiritual transcendence, it is difficult to trace a moment of *givenness* of the modified body that corresponds to the final stage of Christian communion. The secular (perhaps even "profane") practices of body modifiers succeed at figuring an alternative aesthetic that I believe is consistent with the cruciform aesthetic of the Eucharistic community, but they err toward an immanent and ultimately individualistic vision of the redemption of the body (through its various modifications and transformations) without offering the hope of the resurrection.

Moreover, the body is not broken for the redemption of a larger community and therefore fails to offer true *communitas*—while I am not prepared to offer this as a universal critique, it does seem to me that much of the "othering" of body modifiers *may*, at its root, finally be a solipsistic act, rather than living and being *for the Other*. This fracturing is primarily about the individual subject and is likewise, it seems to me, lacking in relational or ethical import (apart from standing in physical, visible protest to the commodifying forces of market and capital in contemporary society). This profound individualism is problematic for a number of reasons. For one thing, body modification is an attempt to liberate the body via practices that in the end paradoxically fall into the trap of the same obsession over the body that they wish to overcome. But more importantly, these practices are completely selfish, individualized, even narcissistic.[19] And so, while taking such pains to create a sense of community amongst body modifiers,

19. See DeMello, Inscription, 150; Featherstone, *Body Modification*, 41–49, Pitts, *In The Flesh*, 194–96.

their rituals are, to some degree, guilty of the criticism directed at them by mainstream society: these are anti-social behaviors, or better for our purposes, they finally reveal themselves as being almost anti-communitarian. Victoria Pitts supports this view when she argues that body mod practices result in "bodies-in-isolation,"[20] but the best evidence I came across is from an interview with Frances Sand, who is something of a celebrity in the body mod subculture.

Frances's mods include facial tattoos (as well as heavy tattooing elsewhere),[21] gauged-out ear, nose, bellybutton and labret piercings, and subdermal implants along her collarbone. In an interview on *BME*, Frances said: "What I do seems to be more spiritual and more personal as time goes on. *I'm feeling an increasing need to be more removed from people too,* just because it's getting harder as I get older to deal with them."[22] Pioneering body modifier Steve Haworth echoes this; when asked what motivates people to undertake extreme mods like subdermal implants, his response was: "Extreme individualism. Ten years ago if you had a piercing or a tattoo you stood alone, [but] today, even though piercing and tattooing are still a wonderful form of self-expression, you stand in a group."[23] In short, the fragmentation indicative of contemporary society is not overcome but is rather reinforced and intensified by this "extreme individualism." Any community or quasi-community that exists is one made up of radical individualists whose bodies transgress boundaries not for the purposes of communion with the other but purely for the self's own sake. This is in stark contrast to what Graham Ward has termed the *transcorporeal* body of Christ, which "becomes eucharistic, because endlessly fractured and fed to others . . . [it] extends in its fracturing, it pluralises as it opens itself toward

---

20. Pitts, *In The Flesh*, 193.

21. Facial tattooing, it should be noted, it still considered very radical by the body mod subculture because regardless of how acceptable tattoos become in mainstream society, tattoos above the neck and especially on the face remain extremely stigmatizing and virtually guarantee that a modified person will be excluded from most aspects of mainstream society; for this reason, facial tattoos are cautioned against, even by the most ardent body mod enthusiasts. In an online interview, Frances Sand has commented: "The facial tattoos . . . I agonized over that thought for a while, it's not something to take on lightly . . . but I didn't want to go back, and I wanted to make sure I never could." See http://www.bmezine.com/news/people/A10101/frances/index.html.

22. Op cit.; my emphasis.

23. Interview with Steve Haworth for *BME*.

an eternal growth. Only as such, can the wounding, can the differences, be redemptive."[24]

SECOND CRITIQUE: WHAT DOES BODY MODIFICATION HAVE TO SAY ABOUT THE EUCHARIST?

Still, I suggest that even body modifiers' tendency toward individualism can serve as a critique of Christian eucharistic practice gone wrong—an indictment of those who participate in communion with selfish intentions or a spirit of disunity. In short, while the parallels deconstruct at certain points, I believe each community and their accompanying rituals both confirm and critique the veracity of the other. Further, I suggest that precisely this sort of plurality of meaning, which can only be achieved through a willingness to attend to the voice of the most radically Other, is necessary to any self-understanding. The Eucharistic community is comprised precisely of modified bodies; perhaps the body modification community could learn from the Church about the implicit sacramentality of their practices if the Church would recognize their inherent connection to every broken body—which includes all of us, really, whether the marks and scars are visible or not—and so suspend judgment long enough to allow the possibility of communion. (This idea of the Eucharist as the basis for the Church's connection to and responsibility for *all bodies*, especially those of the broken, outcast, marginalized, oppressed, etc., is something that was first introduced to me by William Cavanaugh's *Torture and Eucharist*, and I'm still fairly obsessed with more than 10 years later.)

I close with another anecdote from my undergraduate days. I will never forget a theology professor saying to me (to paraphrase): "Until you learn to see the body of a man broken and bloody and hanging from a Cross as the most beautiful image in the world, you fail to understand what the Eucharist is about." What I want to suggest is, in the end, rather simple. I would speculate that if Frances Sand were to be asked her thoughts about contemporary Christianity, she would say something like, "Those are the last people who would ever accept me. I have no use for them; that's why I modify my body. It's my body, my religion." But likewise, if you asked most Christians, regardless of tradition or persuasion, their initial reaction to someone like Frances, they would probably, *at best*, respond, "Well, that's the last person who would ever darken the door of *our* church"—worse

---

24. Ward, *Cities of God*, 95.

responses would involve words like *freak, mutilation, pagan . . . hopeless.* And yet it seems to me that if Christians—and I again include myself here—if *we* really understood the beauty of Christ's *broken* body, and truly believed that Christ's body is given to and for the weak, the marginal, the broken, the outcast, as much (if not more so) as for the healthy, beautiful and powerful, then perhaps we could recognize the beauty, the wholeness, *the person* amidst the longing and need, in these bodies that carry so visibly on their exterior the wounds and the marks of Jesus Christ.

BIBLIOGRAPHY

"About the Church." *Church of Body Modification.* http://uscobm.com/who-are-we/.

Caplan, Jane, editor. *Written On The Body: The Tattoo in European and American History.* London: Reaktion, 2000.

DeMello, Margo. *Bodies of Inscription: A Cultural History of the Modern Tattoo Community.* Durham, NC: Duke University Press, 2003.

Dix, Dom Gregory. *The Shape of the Liturgy.* London and New York: Continuum, 1945.

Featherstone, Mike, editor. *Body Modification.* London, Thousand Oaks and New Delhi: Sage, 2000.

Henderson, Bryan. "Beauty and Inspiration: Frances Sand" (interview). *Body Modification Ezine.* http://news.bme.com/wp-content/uploads/2008/09/pubring/people/A10101/frances/index.html.

"Interview with Steve Haworth." *Body Modification Ezine.* http://news.bme.com/wp-content/uploads/2008/09/pubring/people/A10101/htc.html.

Perkins, Judith. *The Suffering Self: Pain and Narrative Representation in the Early Christian Era.* London: Routledge, 1995

Pitts, Victoria L. *In the Flesh: The Cultural Politics of Body Modification.* Hampshire: Palgrave Macmillan, 2003.

Ricoeur, Paul. *Oneself as Another.* Translated by Kathleen Blamey. Chicago and London: University of Chicago Press, 1992.

"Statement of Faith." *Church of Body Modification.* http://uscobm.com/statement-of-faith/.

Vale, V. ,and Andrea Juno. *Modern Primitives: An Investigation of Contemporary Adornment and Ritual* (Research #12). San Francisco, CA: RE/Search, 1989.

Ward, Graham. *Cities of God.* London: Routledge, 2000.

CHAPTER 8

A Phenomenology of Anorexia Nervosa
What Anorectics Can Teach Us About the Body and the Church

Amanda DiMiele

I REMEMBER THE MOMENT that I realized I was not just on a diet anymore. I was fifteen, underweight in front of my open refrigerator, and coming to terms with the fact that I could not make myself eat. It would take years to recover fully from what I would learn to name as a relatively mild form of anorexia nervosa. It would take even longer to make sense of the experience. Medical science offers both biological and psychological explanations, but the disorder remains mystifying. For example, there is no satisfying answer to what makes some girls vulnerable and others immune, and reliably permanent treatment remains non-existent. A central argument of this paper is that anorexia nervosa remains elusive because anorexic bodies defy the medical model of embodiment. The medicalized body is an object, a machine that is the sum of its parts. Under this model, eating disorders lie in some dysfunction of the machine, typically understood to originate in the brain. The problem is that anorexia is not experienced as a dysfunction. It is experienced as the controlled pursuit of one's own positive ends—typically, the transformation of one's self or one's world. In other words, the experience of anorexia more closely resembles a practical ethic. Medical science simply does not have the conceptual resources to account for anorexia understood this way. For that account, this paper turns to the phenomenology of the body found in the early work of Maurice Merleau-Ponty.

First, though, I must note that I am offering this account not only as a recovered anorectic, but just as importantly, as a Christian. It is incredible to me now that during my experience with anorexia, it never occurred to me that my religion offered me another way to be a body. Every Sunday I affirmed the incarnation and the hope of resurrection in the Apostle's Creed, but nothing about my experience of church forced me to reckon with the implications of these doctrines. I certainly never imagined that they might contradict the understanding of the body I had received from medical discourse. In the words of Merleau-Ponty, then, I am inviting Christians to "rediscover ourselves" by relearning what it means to be a body.[1] That is, I am interested in exploring how a phenomenology of the body might intersect with Christian theology and practice. I am doing this through the specific and particular case of anorexic bodies, but I do so insofar as I believe that they make visible the dis-ease that we all experience in the objectification of our subjective bodies. In other words, anorexic bodies have something to tell us about being human. Thus, I begin this paper by opening a small window into their world through a phenomenological account of anorexic bodies.[2] It is important to note that this account will be specific to anorexia nervosa, a nervous loss of appetite.[3] Historians have identified other forms of anorexia dating back to the 14th century, and I will trace this history to highlight the ways in which medical discourse has shaped modern anorexia. Beneath the obscuring prevalence of the medical model, I argue that the church's thought and practice already offers an alternative way of being body. A phenomenological perspective can help unlock the church's imagination to rediscover the body not as a (dys)functional object,

1. Merleau-Ponty, *Phenomenology of Perception*, 213.

2. I have attempted to use language like "anorexic bodies" instead of "the anorexic body" to acknowledge the truly vast multiplicity of experiences that fall under the name anorexia nervosa. This, of course, makes anorexia very difficult to write about. I have done my best to avoid naming any one experience as *the* experience of some universal "anorexic body." That said, in order to say anything at all I must to some extent generalize. It is a special concern of mine that the reader proceeds understanding that this phenomenological account is descriptive of much of the experience of many anorexic bodies, but certainly not all of them.

3. This, of course, is the medical term. Significantly, it lacks almost any descriptive merits in regard to the actual experience of the disorder, which is marked, if anything, by the intensification of an appetite denied.

but as a subject capable of being in communion with God, creation, and people precisely because it is a body.

A PHENOMENOLOGICAL ACCOUNT OF ANOREXIC BODIES

I am going to focus on two aspects of anorexia nervosa: first, the habits that construct worlds in which the act of eating is possible only under rigidly defined conditions, and second, the isolation of anorexia nervosa. In the first experience, I am gesturing toward one of the hardest things for people who have never experienced anorexia to understand, which is that the inability to eat in given situations is just that: a true inability. This inability goes much deeper than psychological stubbornness. It also goes deeper than biological mechanism. In terms of the latter, it is true that anorectics who have stopped eating entirely do experience withdrawal symptoms if forced to consume food, but they are in the minority. Most anorectics do eat. Caloric intake is at a negative balance, but they still eat comfortably. Their eating, however, is a highly ritualized affair. Some foods are "safe" and therefore edible, but most are not; certain times of day are permissible for eating, but most are not; certain environments and conditions make eating possible, but most do not. The mother of one anorectic, Hannah, describes the (often infuriating) exactitude of these rituals:

> It was the same order with every single meal, every single day. When she'd sit with the vegetables, she'd turn the plate and she'd have three mouthfuls. Then she'd turn the plate and eat three mouthfuls and so on. I'd say to her, "If you're going to eat two bags of vegetables every night, get the big steamer out and cook the whole lot and then sit down and eat with us." But she couldn't because it was too daunting, that much food. She'd have to serve it up in these little portions . . . It nearly drove us bonkers, it really did. It would take her anything up to two and a half hours to eat dinner each night but her total calories was probably only 200 calories. It was mind-blowingly annoying. She knew she was doing it but she couldn't help it.[4]

It is worth noting that this inability to eat in certain contexts is true not only of anorexic women. According to Samantha Murray, many "fat" women report a similar phenomenon when they attempt to eat in public.

4. Halse et al., *Inside Anorexia*, 83.

"It is not simply that the "fat" woman chooses not to eat . . . rather, she literally cannot swallow any food: she has embodied the culturally discursive prohibitions against a "feeding performance" for a woman positioned as "fat" . . . she is ingesting the opinions of others."

Merleau-Ponty's phenomenology of the body makes sense of what is going on in both the case of anorexic and "fat" bodies in these instances. What he writes about the phenomenon of the phantom limb is descriptive also of anorexia: "The refusal of the mutilation . . . [is] not a deliberated decision . . . [is] not of the order of the 'I think that . . .'"[5] I have yet to come across an account of an anorexic person who chose anorexia. Plenty of anorectics come to recognize their anorexia for what it is and then to embrace it, but the inability to eat outside of rigid rules is not a decision. Instead, anorectics, consciously or unconsciously, adopt habits that result in this inability. These habits take the form of rituals that include eating rules, exercise routines, daily mantras to oneself, etc. Adopted in a relatively short space of time, these habits are hugely significant. As Merleau-Ponty writes, in acquiring new habits "the body allows itself to be penetrated by a new signification . . . it [assimilates] a new meaningful core"—a new understanding of the self.[6] This is true even in relatively mundane cases, like that of the typist. Someone who has learned to type "literally incorporates the space of the keyboard into his bodily space." He has understood the keyboard and the act of typing not when he memorizes all of the keys' positions, but when the keyboard becomes an appendage of his own living body. He no longer thinks about it, but acts through it.[7] Critically, this new body knowledge not only provides his body with a new function (typing) but a new way to engage in writing itself and thus, often, thinking. Losing his keyboard would mean an amputation of part of his lived body. He would have to re-learn the act of composing/thinking and who he is as a composer/thinker.

So, anorexic women who adopt new habits are "penetrated by a new signification," a new way of being in the world. This is why women who attempt to give up anorexia, or even chronic dieters who stop dieting, do not experience the loss as the act of liberation in the way that many feminist thinkers cast it. Rather, it is as an act of mourning. As Cressidea Heyes explains, one must mourn the thin or fit self that one desired to be, and

5. Merleau-Ponty, *Perception*, 83.

6. Ibid., 148.

7. Ibid., 146.

more importantly, one must mourn the loss of a context in which it is acceptable to care for the self—to have a discipline to live by.[8] Kirsty, author of the short personal account "Anorexia, My Only Friend," affirms this. She remembers, "[Anorexia] was with me twenty-four hours a day, and it gave me some purpose."[9] Though I consider myself recovered, I still mourn that thin, disciplined person I used to be. When indulging in one too many helpings of dessert, I often catch myself saying wistfully to my husband, "I remember when I had discipline." I am always referring to my anorexic days, and I am never joking.

Perceptual habits function similarly to these motor habits of ritualistic eating. For example, sight itself is a perceptual habit because "vision is nothing without a certain use of the gaze." This is easy to understand in the case of a blind person's cane. She must learn to understand the cane as her own eyes, to perceive through it her world and its pathways, objects, etc. Fascinatingly, Merleau-Ponty writes that people with sight must undergo a similar "acquisition of a certain style of vision."[10] Thus, a report of blind persons who through surgery see for the first time "confirms that [the formerly blind person] sees, but he does not know what he sees . . . He never recognizes his hand as such, he only speaks of a moving white patch." Perhaps the best way, then, to describe the world of an anorectic is to say that she has learned a certain way of seeing—usually herself as fat even when she is thin and, always, the world as full of restrictions and possibilities that simply are not there for most people.

According to Merleau-Ponty, then, the world is no more an abstract, objective space than is the body. He dismisses the idea that the body occupies a "positional spatiality," and instead proposes "situational spatiality."[11] My body is always the origin of the situation and the perception of a place. Something is up because it is above me, expansive because my body takes up so little space within it, fun because it offers concrete actions of play, and so on. Objects, however, also place demands upon me. When I wake up in the morning, my coffee pot solicits me to pour. On the other hand, I hardly notice that I have a coffee pot the rest of the day. This also makes sense of the experience of finding oneself home without remembering the trip there. The corner before Main Street simply solicits

8. Heyes, *Self-Transformations*, 85–87.

9. Shelley, *Anorexics*, 125.

10. Merleau-Ponty, *Perception*, 155.

11. Ibid., 102.

me to turn left. My body responds to this solicitation because "[c]onscious-ness is originally not an 'I think that,' but rather an 'I can.'" That is to say, any given place is less like an abstract grid that bodies are dropped onto and more like theaters of action that bodies inhabit. The meaning of any given place is both limited and opened up by the fact that my body is storied and that these stories are always written in concrete places.

Marya Hornbacher's story epitomizes this concept. Her memoir *Wasted* recounts a nearly life-long struggle with both anorexia and bulimia. At the point in her story that I quote below, she has returned to her parents' house, the home she grew up in, and was managing her eating disorders well. She had been without bulimia (a cycle of binging and purging) for a full year, but the first time she is left alone in the house, she goes to the kitchen and proceeds to binge and purge repeatedly until she passes out. Despite feeling miserable, she does it for the next three days in a row. In the following excerpt, she reflects on why this happened after such a long period of recovery.

> I think it was . . . something so long established that it didn't occur to me *not* to reboot the bulimia. To this day, I cannot stand in my parents' kitchen without thinking about all of the possible foods I might eat. This doesn't happen in my house, or in anyone else's. It is only at my parents' home. I think my eating disorder by that point in my life was pure habit, a habit more deeply ingrained than I or anyone else had thought. I think that merely being alone in my parents' kitchen flipped a switch in my head, and a glaring neon sign started to flash: BINGE.[12]

In the case of Hornbacher, the case of the anorexic girl who can only eat specific foods in specific conditions, and the case of the "fat" woman in public, the same phenomenological principle is in play. Through habits both motor and perceptual we invest the world with meaning pre-reflectively as bodies, and in turn, the world solicits or demands specific responses from us.

Anorexic worlds demand many things, but perhaps most pressing is the demand for isolation. If an anorexic girl is engaged in a starvation diet (defined as 900 calories or less), then she will probably need to hide that fact from her loved ones. She learns to avoid eating around other people. To do that, she has to become good at deceiving people she loves. When she starts to look a little too thin, she will need to guard her body against

---

12. Hornbacher, *Wasted*, 222.

the eyes and touch of other people. She will start wearing baggier clothing and refusing any hugs or bodily contact. Moreover, anorexia is a fundamentally individual pursuit—a demonstration of one's own ability to be in control of her body and other people at will. At the time, all of this tends to feel very safe. One former anorectic, Kate, describes this shrinking of her world: "[Anorexia] made the world easy. You only worried and thought about food and weight. The real world is tough because it means facing tough realities and real fears."[13] The anorectic structures a world defined by predictable rituals and safe from the intrusion of others. And it is incredibly lonely.

MEDICALIZATION AND ANOREXIC BODIES

Anorexia has not always looked like this. In her book *Fasting Girls*, Joan Jacobs Brumberg offers an excellent history of anorexia from the fourteenth through the twentieth century alongside some of the most accurate descriptions of the experience of anorexia nervosa that I have read from a non-anorectic. While she is firm that women's psychology is not fixed over time, she does suggest that the history of anorexia reveals "important continuities in female experience across time and space."[14] She convincingly argues that socio-economic historical conditions have profoundly influenced the experience of anorexic bodies, and she sees a broad movement from sainthood to patienthood. The "sainthood" has its roots in medieval piety. She observes along with Caroline Walker Bynum that for religious medieval women, "food practices provided a basic way to express religious ideals of suffering and service to their fellow creatures." Thus, the kinds of behavior moderns associate with anorexia nervosa were understood by medieval saints and their contemporaries as anorexia mirabilis—a miraculous loss of appetite. Anorexia was a miracle because medieval religious persons believed that by overcoming the appetites, one is freed to love God and serve neighbor without distraction. These holy anorectics never describe anorexia as something they "suffered" in the sense that moderns use it—as being afflicted by an external force beyond one's control. Rather, the saints exclusively use the language of suffering in a positive sense, as a participation in the suffering of Christ and thus an avenue to intimacy with God and the suffering bodies of other people.

13. Shelley, *Anorexics*, 17.
14. Brumburg, *Fasting Girls*, 5.

Victorian spirituality favored a mind-body dualism (privileging the former) and so also tended to look on anorexic behavior—this form of anorexia simply called "fasting girls"—as a gift. This was also the time, Brumberg notes, in which both clergy and physicians started investigating cases of holy fasting. This competition for authority over the body "marked the beginning" of medicalization.[15] By the eighteenth century, abstinence from food was considered a medical problem, and hardly a spiritual miracle or curse.[16] By the twentieth century, the science of nutrition had so advanced that "the rules of feeding and eating were codified and women had a moral responsibility to learn the catechism."[17] In his book *Food, Morals and Meaning*, John Coveney convincingly argues that still today nutrition discourse provides both a host of problems around which individuals problematize their own existence, and it provides an ethics according to which individuals can shape their lives.[18]

In all of this I do not mean to villify medical practitioners. As Rosalyn Diprose has said, "The medical reduction and production [of a normalized, objective body] is often as unwitting as it is powerful." But it is powerful. When the church does not claim authority in discussions of what the body is for, the body is inscribed with other meanings and purposes. As Brumberg puts it, "Sadly, the cult of diet and exercise is the closest thing our secular society offers women in terms of a coherent philosophy of the self."[19] I found this to be true of my own experience. Part of the panic of that revelation in front of my refrigerator had to do with the fact that I was becoming aware that I did not want to be an anorexic body anymore, but I could not imagine an alternative that met my emotional needs in the way anorexia did. In the short term, becoming a competitive runner was what saved me. I started running as an anorectic, but becoming a runner meant a whole new set of habits—an entirely new identity and community—that required, among other changes, that I take in more "fuel."

My body could only sustain competitive running for a few years before a string of injuries finally forced me to take an early retirement. I found myself then asking the same questions I had asked before. Why were these experiences—losing my anorexia, losing my ability to run—so traumatic?

15. Ibid., 51.
16. Ibid., 57.
17. Ibid., 235.
18. Coveney, *Food*, 23.
19. Brumberg, *Fasting Girls*, 10, 165.

What other options for embracing my bodily existence were open to me? The difference this time was that I had begun studying religion, and it occurred to me that theology ought to have something to say about the body.

THE CHURCH'S COMPLICITY IN MEDICALIZATION

Theology, of course, has a great deal to say about the body. All too often, though, theology at both the popular and academic levels is complicit in medicalization. This was certainly my experience of church, and I think it is most people's experience. French Catholic philosopher Jacques Maritain asserted this complicity quite bluntly when he wrote that the church could speak directly only to the spiritual realm, while "over temporal things the church has an indirect power, but only as those things affect the spiritual order of salvation of souls."[20] It is worth noting that in the book *Torture and Eucharist*, William Cavanaugh traced the enormous influence of Maritain's philosophy to the tragedy that took place under the dictator Pinochet in Chile. When Chilean bodies began disappearing to be tortured, the church was initially paralyzed. The Catholic Church was finally able to resist by rediscovering its authority over the body. Its tactics included excommunication (i.e., denial of the body of Jesus in the Eucharist to torturers) and the issuing of a document entitled "I Am Jesus, Whom You Are Persecuting." That is, the church understood the body of Christ as participating in the suffering of the bodies that were tortured by Pinochet's regime.[21]

In my own experience, the church in America has reclaimed no such authority or imagination over the body. I most often witness the label "stewardship" being tacked onto healthy living campaigns: i.e., God gave you your body, so make sure you maintain the gift and keep it functioning well by following the recommendations of medical discourse. One might as well substitute the word "body" for "car." Implicit in this logic is that medicine has authority over the body, since the only thing "Christian" about this is the motivation. The habits and the *telos* still belong to medical discourse. This becomes dangerous when medical and Christian purposes contradict one another. Granted, the *telos* of the body in medical discourse is rarely, if ever, stated overtly. Certainly, however, medical discourse is concerned with health, and common arguments for national/global health are utilitarian—e.g., overall health reduces health care costs for everyone. That

20. Cavanaugh, *Torture*, 159.

21. Ibid.,111.

is not untrue. But it implicitly makes immoral (or at least problematically "abnormal") the bodies of the disabled, of the chronically ill, of the elderly, and of the poor who lack the time and money to buy and cook nutritious food, much less see a doctor—in other words, the kinds of bodies that Jesus seems most concerned with in the gospels.

Just as concerning, a main goal of the medicalized body is to remain functioning—to avoid death and suffering—for as long as possible. Again, that goal is not inherently bad. Suffering in and of itself ought not to be valorized. But there are greater ends than health. For followers of a Christ who willingly suffered in order to defeat death, the level of importance that medical discourse invests in health makes little sense as a Christian *telos*. When we forget this, we start seeing parishioners more worried about sharing germs than they are about sharing Holy Communion.[22] This comes in stark contrast to St. Catherine of Siena, a holy anorectic. While tending the sick, Catherine was repulsed by a woman's cancerous sores. Ashamed of her repulsion toward a body she was supposed to be loving, she drank a ladle full of pus from the sores in order to overcome her disgust.[23] This is the difference between a medicalized imagination and a thoroughly Christian imagination. The former is about self-preservation. The latter is about loving and serving others.

The church's complicity in medicalization is perhaps most blatant in the proliferation of "devotional" dieting literature. Books labeled "Christian life and spirituality" made up about 40 percent of self-help books in 2004, and a significant number of those books revolved around diet and weight loss.[24] Christian diet support groups also abound, and millions of Christians consider weight loss a key part of Christian discipleship. Unfortunately, "their reflections on this point have rarely gone deeper than affirming that because the body is God's temple, being slender is part of living the true Christian life."[25] Other attempts at theological reflection have

22. Granted, some people have legitimate reasons for this worry—people suffering a disease that radically lowers their immune system, for instance. Most of the concern, however, is not legitimate. This has become such a great concern for so many churches in the Methodist tradition that a denomination-sanctioned curriculum on the Eucharist in the United Methodist Church felt the need to devote several paragraphs to defending the use of a common loaf and cup against the fear of germs. See Felton, *Holy Mystery*, 54.

23. Bell, *Holy Anorexia*, 25.

24. Griffith, *Born Again Bodies*, 2. Some of the titles included in that number over the years are *Slim For Him* (1980), *"Help Lord, The Devil Wants Me Fat!"* (1982), *Pray Your Weight Away* (1952), and *More of Jesus, Less of Me* (1976)—to name just a few.

25. Griffith, *Born Again* Bodies, 180.

included arguments that people who are not thin and fit are not good representatives of Christ. (As Murray notes, people never simply perceive a "fat" person. In the act of perceiving, people produce an [unfair] identity around the "fat" person: laziness, lack of control, gluttony, greed, and asexuality.[26]) Aside from these arguments, and a heavy rhetoric equating fat with sin, "devotional dieters [in the 1980s] were in full unison with the American diet culture surrounding them . . . [and before long], identical norms for health and beauty were simply assumed to apply to Christians and heathens alike."[27] Obviously this is not true of all Christians or churches in America, but given how dominant it is, is it any wonder that few anorexic accounts conclude with having found an alternative understanding of bodies in Christianity?

REDISCOVERING THE BODY AS CHRISTIANS

The church ought to be the place where people are unavoidably confronted with a different way to imagine being a body. For example, everything that (rightly or wrongly) falls under the header of "New Age" connotes mind/body practices. In the same way, Christianity ought to evoke a specific and unique set of bodily practices that point to a specific and unique understanding of the body itself. We ought to think of Christianity this way because of what is already given in the church. To name a few of these givens: the sacraments revolve around the lived body in the world—eating and drinking in Eucharist, bathing in baptism, joining together two bodies in marriage, laying on hands in the anointing of the sick and in ordination, etc. Christian hope lies not in escaping our bodies, but in the resurrection of our bodies; we have the radical doctrines of the incarnation, resurrection, and ascension of Christ; as a church, we claim to be the body of Jesus on earth; a concern for the poor necessarily means a concern for the bodies of the poor.[28] Examples abound. Nevertheless, the average layperson (or even pastor) continues to assume a basic dualism between self and body

26. Murray, *Female Body*, 72.

27. Griffith, *Born Again Bodies*, 170, 186.

28. Matthew 25:35–40 (NRSV): "'for I was hungry and you gave me food, I was thirsty and you gave me something to drink, I was a stranger and you welcomed me, I was naked and you gave me clothing, I was sick and you took care of me, I was in prison and you visited me.' Then the righteous will answer him, 'Lord, when was it that we saw you hungry and gave you food [. . .]' and the king will answer them, 'Truly I tell you, just as you did it to one of the least of these who are members of my family, you did it to me.'"

that privileges the emotional experiences of the supposedly non-material soul over the material realities of being in the world.

Reimagining the body thus begins with an appreciation for the kinds of arguments that Merleau-Ponty puts forth. Most basically, Christians need to start talking about bodies as what we are: we live as bodies. We will die as bodies. We will be resurrected as bodies. There is no scenario in which *we are* without it also being true that *we are bodies.* The very practical implications of this include the conviction that Christian practice and discipline is not for achieving some pure or spiritual state, where "pure" and "spiritual" are understood to mean "non-material." If anything, Christian discipline is for bringing us back into our bodies—for making us the kind of people capable of being in concrete relationship with others and with creation. Following on that, loving God, neighbor, and self does not mean harboring warm feelings generally. It means loving bodies (our own and others) and the material *stuff* of creation that sustains them. We love bodies as Christians when we are not afraid to be touched by them. We hold the stiff, gnarled hand; we embrace the person who could use a shower; we lay hands on the sick person; we get soil under our fingernails in a community garden; above all, we share a common cup with whoever decides to walk through the doors of the church Sunday morning. Just as crucially, we are also the recipients of all this, letting our hands be held and our bodies embraced. As Christians, it ought to be apparent to us that our bodies are not the boundary between us, but that by which we are in communion with God, other people, and the world.

This idea that the body is that which enables communion is almost impossible under a mechanistic model of embodiment. Anorexia nervosa teaches us that. Medieval saints with anorexia mirabilis, saturated in a Christian imagination of the body, understood food practices (including abstinence from food) as a means of being with and serving others. The "nervous" anorectic's life, by contrast, is marked by isolation and the necessarily individual pursuit of "salvation." She cuts herself off in her imagination from the lived body that makes her human. I claimed already that anorexic bodies tell us something about being human. I would add that the particular case of anorexia nervosa should haunt Christians with the danger of surrendering authority over the body to discourses that mechanize and individualize it.

FUTURE DIRECTIONS

Practically speaking, I am not suggesting that every church start a Sunday school class on Merleau-Ponty's phenomenology (though I certainly would not stop any churches interested). I do think that the intersection of phenomenology and theology can help pastors and other church leaders better communicate just how radically different this Christian way of imagining the body is to the mechanized models that dominate our culture. A new way of imagining bodies in the church begins with teaching leaders and laypeople alike, with or without explicit reference to Merleau-Ponty, to think about bodies differently. Once we manage this, the harder question becomes how to incorporate these concepts into our lived bodies such that it becomes a perceptual habit, a part of our pre-reflective understanding. Emphasizing the sacraments, like encouraging more churches to celebrate Eucharist weekly (even daily), is a basic first step. Much more will be needed to overcome today's barrage of mechanizing discourse, and many more conversations in that vein are waiting to be had.

Dealing specifically with anorexic bodies, there is one caveat for this and future work, and that is that I do not suggest that in reimagining embodiment, the church will "fix" anorexia. Anorexia is far too complex to each person to be so predictable. Still, I do think this Christian reimagining could be incredibly helpful for many anorectics—it would have been for me. Moreover, in reassigning to the church authority over the body, I do not mean to say that medicine has no authority. It certainly does, and many anorectics need its help. In this paper I have only argued that medicine does not have *exclusive* or *primary* authority over the body.

Finally, there remains the question, implicitly raised already in this paper, of how to understand other forms of anorexia. For the reasons I have mentioned, there is nothing redemptive in the modern experience of anorexia *nervosa*. To drive that point home, I contrasted anorexia nervosa with anorexia mirabilis, arguing that the latter, under a Christian imagination of the body, served to connect women to God and to people as an act of piety and service. Undeniably, this suggests that anorexia mirabilis is in some way a good. This was not a problematic claim in a time when health was understood as less of a moral imperative and suffering was not understood as inherently bad. Still, I hesitate to say that anorexia in any form can be a positive spiritual discipline. This is part of the broader question of how Christians ought to understand the history of extreme asceticism within the church. Are the practices of the Desert Fathers "unhealthy" traditions that we should denounce, or is that judgment merely the voice of medical discourse speaking from deep within our perceptual habits?

For now I leave these questions open. I began this paper with an invitation to Christians to rediscover ourselves. That has been my hope in writing this paper, a hope best articulated in the full quote from which I drew the invitation: "We have learned again to sense our bodies; we have discovered, beneath objective and detached knowledge of the body, this other knowledge that we have of it because it is always with us and because we are bodies . . . by reestablishing contact with the body and with the world . . . we will also rediscover ourselves."[29] Christians have much to rediscover.

29. Merleau-Ponty, *Perception*, 213.

BIBLIOGRAPHY

Anorexics on Anorexia. Edited by Rosemary Shelley. Philadelphia: Jessica Kingsley Publishers, 1997.

Bell, Rudolph. *Holy Anorexia*. Chicago: University of Chicago Press, 1987.

Brumberg, Joan Jacobs. *Fasting Girls: The History of Anorexia Nervosa*. New York: Vintage Books, 2000.

Cavanaugh, William T. *Torture and Eucharist*. Malden, MA: Blackwell, 2008.

Coveney, John. *Food, Morals and Meaning: The Pleasure and Anxiety of Eating*. New York: Routledge, 2000.

Diprose, Rosalyn. *Corporeal Generosity: On Giving with Neitzsche, Merleau-Ponty, and Levinas*. New York: State University of New York Press, 2002.

Griffith, R. Marie. *Born Again Bodies: Flesh and Spirit in American Christianity*. Los Angeles: University of California Press, 2004.

Halse, Christine, et. al. *Inside Anorexia: The Experiences of Girls and Their Families*. Philadelphia: Jessica Kingsley Publishers, 2008.

Hornbacher, Marya. *Wasted: A Memoir of Anorexia and Bulimia*. New York: Harper Collins, 1998.

Merleau-Ponty, Maurice. *Phenomenology of Perception*. Trans. Donald A. Landes. New York: Routledge, 2012.

Murray, Samantha. *The 'Fat' Female Body*. New York: Palgrave MacMillan, 2008.

CHAPTER 9

Listening to the Silence Surrounding Nonconventional Bodies

Teri Merrick

IN HIS BEAUTIFULLY WRITTEN essay "The Body's Grace," Rowan Williams invites his reader to shift her perspective on decisions about sexual activity away from the usual legal and ethical to a concern about what we want our sexual lives to say:

> How much do we want our sexual activity to communicate? How much do we want it to display a breadth of human possibility and a sense of the body's capacity to heal and enlarge the life of others?[1]

In this essay, I am inviting my reader to make a similar shift to the hermeneutical perspective and consider: How much do we want our reception of nonconventional bodies to communicate? How much do we want it to display about the body's capacity to heal and enlarge our life together? However, before we can adequately address these questions, we need to consider what we currently communicate, and the primary mode of that communication is silence.

The narratives of intersex and transgender people bear witness that their reception into the world and various communities is overwhelming

1. Williams, "The Body's Grace," 313.

marked by silence, silence of all kinds. Their reception in Christian church-es and religious academic institutions in the United States is often the same. Consider my own story. I am chair of a Theology and Philosophy depart-ment at a self-described evangelical Wesleyan institution. In August 2013, my colleague and former chair, Professor Adam Ackley (previously known as Heather Clements) asked me into his office and explained that he was a transgender male. On the advice of his medical team, he was discontinuing the pharmaceutical and psychiatric care of the past twenty years aimed at trying to feminize him. This past treatment protocol, as Adam and those of us who worked with him can attest, had resulted in deteriorating health to a point that became life-threatening. As a courtesy, he wanted to alert me to the fact that he was beginning the medical and legal transition enabling him to align his gender presentation with his gender identity. To make a long story short, the various and conflicting details of which can be dis-covered by doing a quick Google search, Adam agreed to be relieved of his teaching and faculty duties on October 4th, 2013.

Throughout this five-week stretch, I witnessed all sorts of silence. Speaking for myself, the silences were primarily tear-your-hair-out mad-dening, punctuated with still moments of hope, despair, anger, and even-tually resolve. For Adam, I can safely report that the silences most often communicated abandonment, rejection, and sometimes outright hostil-ity. Yet, there were also moments of quiet, shared grief and affirmation. Most perplexing of all, however, was that these silences occurred despite sincere, oft-repeated and explicitly stated desires on the part of university administrators to engage in "thoughtful conversations" about transgender generally and Adam's employment situation in particular.[2] We have all experienced the fact that what gets transmitted via linguistic signs—words, gestures, and even silences—is often more than and sometimes contradicts the intended meaning of an author or a speaker. But when the mismatches between what we *want* to say and what *is* said persist and multiply, this begs for an explanation. It further suggests that arriving at a complete ex-planation will require not only examining the inner-workings of individual psyches, but also the socio-linguistic dynamics of a group.

In her seminal work in the theology of disability, Nancy Eiesland points out that many well-intentioned Christian communities engage in a kind of "double-speak" when it comes to addressing nonconventional

2. Joint Statement approved by Dr. H. A. Ackley and Azusa Pacific University and released for public distributing on October 4, 2013.

bodies. She notes that in 1980 the General Convention of American Lutheran Church (ALC) passed a resolution to "address the attitudinal, architectural, and communication barriers that prevent full access by persons with disabilities."[3] Yet, five years later the ALC stated that people with so-called significant physical and mental disabilities were not eligible for ordination. Eiesland offers several reasons as to why the ALC could not authentically and consistently practice its stated policy of extending complete access to people with disabilities. The reasons most relevant to my purposes are, first, the perpetuation of an individual model of disability and, second, continually "locating able-bodied people at the 'speaking center.'"[4]

Eiesland explains that the individual model conceives of disability primarily as a dysfunctional or malformed property of an individual. Care for people with disabilities then aims at providing the biomedical, psychological and vocational resources necessary for remedying or managing their dysfunction, thereby affording them access to the goods available in various communities and institutions. She argues that this model of analysis is limited insofar as it neglects the fact that much of the social isolation experienced by people with disabilities is due to long-standing, society-wide prejudice and discrimination. Therefore, the exclusion and marginalization of nonconventional bodies cannot be fully understood or remedied unless one moves to a minority-group model of analysis.

On Eiesland's minority-group model, one distinguishes between impairment, disability and handicap. "Impairment" refers to an atypical bodily configuration constituting the actual loss of a physiological form or function. "Disability" refers to the inability to perform some task or role because of an impairment. "Handicap" refers to a social disadvantage that occurs because of an impairment or disability.[5] Drawing these distinctions enables us to recognize that some disabilities and handicaps are not the direct result of an impairment, but rather the result of societal attitudes concerning that impairment. This in turn opens up the possibility of redressing these disabilities and handicaps by challenging and changing discriminatory attitudes and practices.[6]

I contend that among the discriminatory practices that Eiesland describes is the practice of not allowing intersex and transgender bodies a

3. Eiesland, *Disabled God*, 76.

4. Ibid., 77.

5. Ibid., 27.

6. Ibid.

voice within the speaking center of Wesleyan churches or universities. Intersex and transgender people may be talked *about* or *at*, but they are rarely or never directly heard *from*. My hope in what follows is to begin redressing this problem by attending to the testimonies of intersex and transgender people or, more specifically, to hear what they have heard in the silences surrounding them.

The pervasiveness of this silence is evidenced by the fact that so few people outside of those working in specialized areas within biomedicine and psychology know what the terms "intersex" or "transgender" actually refer to. Moreover, it is only because practitioners within these fields started listening to their intersex and transgender patients that these designations and their respective treatment protocols recently underwent substantial modification. "Intersex" refers to variations in the biological markers of sexual identity—chromosomes, gonads, hormones or anatomical structure—such that not all of these markers line up under a strict male or female classification.[7] So, for example, one out of 20,000 people born with forty-six XY chromosomes are androgen insensitive. Since androgen is a hormone contributing to the development of internal and external male genitalia, these babies are born as genetic or chromosomal males, but with phenotypes ranging from a typically appearing female body to bodies with increasing degrees of ambiguity.[8] The incidence figures of live intersex births vary, depending on what variations are classed as intersex. However, one out of 2500 births is an oft-repeated and reputable figure, which means that the number of intersex births equals those born with cystic fibrosis.[9]

In 2005, the International Consensus Conference on Intersex was held in Chicago. This was the culmination of years of advocacy by intersex people asking that the medical community listen to their testimony about the prevailing treatment paradigm for intersex patients and their families. The conference was noteworthy not only for explicitly "recognizing and accepting the place of patient advocacy," but also for inviting Bo Laurent (Cheryl Chase) and another intersex person to sit at the table alongside forty-eight medical experts to craft a new, more-patient centered protocol.[10]

7. Arboleda and Vilain, "Disorders of Sex Development," 351. See too UK Intersex Association, "UKIA Guide to Intersex."

8. Ibid., 366.

9. See Cornwall, "Intersex Conditions (DSDs) and Pastoral Care" for a discussion of these incidence figures.

10. Lee et al., "Consensus Statement," 491.

The result was the publication of "Consensus Statement of Management of Intersex Disorders," *Clinical Guidelines for the Management of Disorders of Sex Development in Childhood* and *Handbook for Parents*. These publications are now widely recommended for clinicians, parents, intersex people and anyone interested in what it means to be or to care for an intersex person.

Compared to the ALC's 1980 General Conference and its resolutions concerning people with disabilities, the Consensus Conference and its subsequent publications appear to be models of engaging in a constructive and collaborative dialogue between a hitherto speaking center of conventionally bodied institutional elites and those on the margins. However, advocacy groups like the UK Intersex Association have denounced the conference and its presumed consensus. They claim that the intersex people were not sufficiently represented and that the proposed nomenclature change from "intersex" to "disorders of sexual development" perpetuates the stigma and shaming of intersex bodies.[11] I will argue that the Conference and resultant documents implicitly retain an individual model of analysis. That is, they fail to examine and develop a strategy for responding to inhospitable and discriminatory societal attitudes and practices targeted at bodies that cannot be strictly classed as male or female. Once we turn to the narratives of parents of intersex children, we will see that failure to change such attitudes and practices makes it highly unlikely that parents will opt for the treatment called for in the new *Guidelines*.

"Transgender" is an adjective that refers to experiencing oneself as possessing a gender identity different from the sex or gender identity that was assigned, an assignment usually occurring at birth.[12] Unlike intersex, the genetic factors contributing to the incongruity between the gender identity experienced by the transgender child and their sex or gender assignment have not yet been identified.[13] Recent research, however, indicates that the brain exhibits distinctive sex markers of its own. Neurogeneticists cite evidence that the brain develops sexual differences prior to and independently of the presence of gonadal hormones like testosterone.[14] This has

11. The United Kingdom Intersex Association, "Why not 'Disorders of Sex Development.'"

12. See GLAAD, "An Ally's Guide to Terminology" and the American Psychological Association, *DSM*-V, 451.

13. Cornwall "Intersex, Identity, Disability Project Briefing Paper 3."

14. See T. C. Ngun et al., "The Genetics of Sex Differences" and G. Rametti et al. "White matter microstructure."

led to the hypothesis that a transgender identity may be due to the brain taking a path of sexual development differing from that taken by the rest of the body. In other words, it may turn out that transgender is yet another type of variation in embryonic sexual development and would thus fall under the broader category of intersex.

Although there is no conclusive evidence of the genetic basis for transgender at this particular time, it is important to note that the American Academy of Pediatrics and the American Psychological Association (APA) already reject social constructivist theories of gender, which neglect the substantial role biological factors play in sex and gender development.[15] There is also plenty of evidence that transgender children and adults experience a profound sense of alienation, both in relation to their own sexually developing bodies and in relation to societal norms requiring them to conform to their gender assignment. Consider Adam's own testimony of the alienation experienced as a transgender male:

> I have always been a spiritual seeker, and I have always felt differently gendered than the people around me. These things intersected for me since childhood, where my private conversations with a God I wasn't really sure existed were all I had to help me survive childhood experiences of feeling unsafe, ashamed, and secretive about almost every aspect of my gender and sexuality . . . I became a Christian at eighteen. However, it soon became clear that affiliating with Christian community would mean increasing my efforts to conform to the female gender identity assigned to me socially since birth rather than pursuing the medical transition I had first thought possible for myself back when tennis star Renee Richards came out successfully as a male-to-female transgender celebrity during my childhood . . . To that end [trying "harder to be a good Christian woman, wife and mother"], various doctors treated me with a host of female hormones and psychiatric medications for decades, though nothing worked. I became increasingly suicidal, and like 47 percent of all transgender people, I attempted suicide.[16]

Adam rightly stresses that this is *his* story, "one of many very diverse stories on the spectrum of transgender identity."[17] Still, the strong desire for a body congruent with one's gender identity, the intense, internalized pressure to

15. See APA, *DSM-5*, 451; and Karkazis, *Fixing Sex*, 63–86.

16. Ackley, "Transgender and Christian," 1.

17. Ibid.

conform to exclusively disjunctive male or female societal norms, and the self-loathing, self-medicating and self-abuse that result when efforts at congruence or conformity are made or imposed are common experiences of transgender people.[18] The APA now diagnoses and treats this experience as a case of "gender dysphoria," rather than a case of "gender identity disorder," since it is the dysphoria, not the "identity per se," that is the cause of a transgender person's psychosocial distress.[19] Lastly, we need a term for those who, so far as they know, are neither intersex nor transgender. I will use the modifier "invariantly sex and cisgender" to refer to such people.

Having fixed our use of terms, let us return to our primary question: why all silence surrounding intersex and transgender bodies and what does it mean? When reading the narratives of intersex people and their parents, the type of silence that immediately comes to the fore is what I call "the silence of authorized care." Under the treatment guidelines developed by psychologist John Money and the John Hopkins School of Medicine in the 1950s, parents of intersex children were encouraged not to tell the child or anyone else about their intersex condition. This discursive strategy was driven by the belief of Money and other researchers that although gender identity and sex-specific behavior was due to both biological and sociological factors, socialization was the dominant influence, particularly during early childhood.[20] Clinicians reasoned that if a child began life assuming an invariant sex identity, if surgery and hormone therapy were used to reduce the observable degree of variance and if the social milieu in which the child was raised reinforced the sex and gender assignment, the child too would accept it. Because the treatment protocols inspired by Money et al. focus on achieving a stable, cisgender identity and advocate for infant reconstructive surgery as a means of approximating invariant sex and gender presentation, this approach is referred to as "the optimal gender theory" and contrasted with "the informed consent approach" advocated those opposing infant cosmetic surgery.[21]

18. Ecklund, "Intersectionality in Children: A Case Study," 256–64.

19. American Psychological Association (2013), 451–59.

20. Karkazis, *Fixing Sex,* 52–55. It should be noted that Money himself advocated that intersex children should be told the truth about their diagnoses and subsequent treatment when it was age-appropriate. However, based on interviews with clinicians and parents and the narratives of intersex people having undergone these treatments, it is clear that silence and secrecy was practiced as much if not more than age-appropriate mutual open communication (ibid., 59–60).

21. Sanders et al. "Searching for harmony," 2221.

It is important to recognize that the silence encouraged under the optimal gender theory is intended to protect a child from experiencing the very kind of somatic and social alienation that Adam describes. And it is this same need to protect their child that parents most often cite when opting for the silence of authorized care. The authors of a 2011 article in the *Journal of Advanced Nursing* analyzing parent narratives report:

> Many parents reflected that 'not telling anyone' became a mechanism, by which they could protect their child's genital uncertainty from scrutiny and curiosity yet conversely this secrecy increased their anxiety.[22]

One thing to note about this report is that although Money's guidelines were standard practice up through 2005, this is no longer the case. The new treatment guidelines emerging from 2005 Consensus Conference urge caution in deciding on early genital reconstructive surgery. Studies show that these surgeries run the risk of the loss of sexual sensitivity and there is the likelihood of repeated surgeries to meet the desired cosmetic outcome and ensure reliable sexual functioning. There is also little data to support the idea that these surgeries actually improve a patient's sexual functioning or quality of life. Further, in contrast to the earlier guidelines, the recommended protocol now explicitly and unambiguously calls for "open communication with patients and families."[23] It is unclear whether the parents interviewed in this report were advised in accordance with the optimal gender theory or the new guidelines.

What is clear is that even when parents planned on telling the child of their condition, they still opted for silence towards others as a means of presenting their child as invariantly sex and cisgender so as to protect them from embarrassment or being ostracized:

> My husband wouldn't have told a soul, no one would have known. It would have been a secret, nothing mentioned because it is genitalia and it is still looked at as something that's taboo (Maria).[24]

> If everybody accepted that everybody's different, it isn't a problem. But people don't accept that everybody's different. You have to conform to the way that the public says you should be (Andrea).[25]

22. Ibid., 2224.
23. Lee et al., "Consensus Statement," e490.
24. Sanders et al "Searching for harmony," 2224.
25. Ibid., 2225.

Sadly, parents' anticipation that their child would be stigmatized was sometimes confirmed:

> When you've got people stopping you in the street, pulling the covers back off you're baby and it's like, 'oh you'd never know would ya?' Never know what, 'you know that your child's basically a freak,' you know . . . I actually got beaten up (Faye).

Throughout these narratives, it is obvious that the parents' silence is intended to express care, love and affirmation of their child. Drawing on my own experience and the anecdotal evidence shared by others, it is fair to say that at least some of the institutional silence of Wesleyan churches and universities is similarly motivated.

Is this then what the silence of authorized care means? Does it say that intersex and transgender people are welcomed and loved? My answer is "no" and here is why. If you have been married as long as I have, then you have probably heard "That may have been what you meant, but it wasn't what you said." You have also had to admit the truth of this claim. To the extent that the purpose of a linguistic sign is to communicate something, the something being communicated depends as much on what the intended audience hears as it does on what the speaker intends. As we will see, the pervasive and prevailing silence surrounding their bodies communicates neither care, nor love nor affirmation to intersex or transgender people.

So what have intersex children and adults heard from the silence of authorized care? Simply put, that they and their bodies are unmentionable shames. Sherrie G. Morris is a San Diego lawyer with complete androgen insensitivity (AIS) who underwent Money's optimal gender treatment protocol. For Sherrie, her parents' and practitioners' silence communicated that her body was "a tragic mistake of nature"[26] and that she was "a one-off freak."[27] She writes:

> If I had a choice, I would not elect to be born without AIS. The challenges that I have faced have contributed to who I am. Having AIS is not for me the tragedy my parents and doctors thought it would be. Secrecy and silence have left far deeper scars than my transitory struggle to come to terms with having been born with testes and XY chromosomes. Having met hundreds of other women of AIS, I can say that this has been true for them as well.[28]

26. Morris, "Twisted Lies," 4.
27. Ibid., 6.
28. Ibid., 11–12.

Numerous interviews and narratives of intersex people confirm that what Sherrie heard they too have heard. Regardless of its intention, the silence of authorized care tells them that their bodies are shameful and monstrous. Having conducted extensive interviews with fifty-three clinicians, researchers, intersex adults and parents of intersex children, Katrina Karkazis aptly summarizes the outcome of this discursive strategy:

> Ironically, the attempt by some parents to spare their children anxiety by keeping information from them and not discussing their condition may in fact have exacerbated these feelings, creating the impression that the child's body was unspeakably abnormal.[29]

So, if the intent is to express love and support for intersex and transgender people, then the predominate type of silence issuing from the authorized speakers in biomedical, ecclesial and academic circles is a distorted form of communication, for it repeatedly misfires and says the exact opposite of what is intended.

This conclusion raises the question as to who is really being addressed in this silence. To answer this question, we must heed Eiesland's advice and adopt a minority-group model of discursive analysis. For Eiesland, a group of people qualifies as a minority-group if "their physical or cultural characteristics" single them out "from others in the society in which they live for differential and unequal treatment."[30] She points out that the prejudice directed at people with disabilities or nonconventional bodies usually manifests itself in a "subtle form of pervasive paternalism and social aversion" rather than "overt bigotry and violence."[31] When it comes to transgender people, there is no doubt that they meet Eiesland's criteria. Adam's case is just one of many that could be cited to show that transgender people encounter differential and unequal treatment within our society. I also assume that my reader will grant that transgender people are often targets of both subtle and overt forms of prejudice. It may not be as obvious that cases like Sherrie's also satisfy Eiesland's criteria, but this is only because people with AIS and other variations in their biological sex markers can attempt to hide these variations and pass as invariantly sexed. Indeed, the treatment protocols and concerns expressed in parental testimonies would be inexplicable were it not for the fact that the nonconventional physical character-

29. Karkazis, "Fixing Sex," 220.
30. Eiesland, *Disabled God*, 63.
31. Ibid., 64.

istics of intersex children and adults do single them out for differential and unequal treatment in the societies in which they live. Moreover, as I have been arguing throughout, the silence of authorized care is precisely how a prejudicial pervasive paternalism and social aversion is communicated to intersex people.

Once we apply minority-group model of analysis, one can see that this silence is in fact a highly effective discursive strategy. Throughout this communicative act, nonconventional bodies remain at the discursive margins. The sender of this silence is the authorized voice of an invariantly sex and cisgender speaking center and it is addressing itself, trying to calm its own fears and aversions. By recognizing who and what is being actually being addressed, this silence can now be interpreted as better expressing what was intended, for what it says is "this body is no cause for alarm because it fits well within the established invariant dimorphic sex and gender order of things." Ironically and tragically, therefore, the silence ends up reinforcing the very prejudicial and discriminatory societal attitudes and practices that clinicians and parents sought to protect children from.

In defending the decision to replace the term "intersex" with "disorders of sex development" (DSD), the crafters and proponents of the Consensus Statement maintain that this change was necessary to avoid the "negative social connotation" of the former.[32] They argue that this negative connotation was potentially harmful to some patients and produced confusion in parents and practitioners alike.[33] Here is where the problem of remaining within an individual model of diagnostic analysis is seen most acutely. The recommended treatment protocols and discursive strategies urged the Consensus Conference never challenge societal attitudes and institutional practices stigmatizing and marginalizing intersex or transgender bodies. But unless these attitudes and practices are challenged, it is extremely unlikely that the new treatment protocols for both intersex and transgender children, calling for open mutual dialogue between patients, parents and clinicians and the need to build authentically affirming supportive communities, will actually be implemented.

Recall Eiesland's distinction between impairment, disability and handicap. One issue that I have not tried to tackle here is that the extent to which variations in sex and gender markers should be considered

---

32. Arboleda and Vilain "Disorders of Sex Development," 351. See too Lee et al., "Consensus Statement," e488.

33. Ibid.

impairments at all. Based on what I have said, however, we can conclude that the most charitable interpretation of the silence of authorized care is that it is a discursive strategy intended to remedy the disabilities and handicaps experienced by intersex and transgender children and adults. That is, it aims to afford them access to the functions and roles available to typically configured male or female bodies and to minimize the social disadvantages accruing because they play, study, work and worship in places that can only accommodate invariantly sex and cisgender people. As we have seen, however, this strategy fails to adequately attain its objective. Like the ALC's 1980 resolution, the protocols arising from 2006 General Conference, the APA's DSM-V, and the public declarations of Wesleyan institutions expressing the intent to engage in a constructive and collaborative dialogue with those on margins cannot be actualized so long as we persist in speaking a silence telling transgender and intersex people that their bodies are tragic mistakes of nature necessitating medical intervention and unspeakable objects necessitating Christian charity.

I began by inviting my reader to consider what we would like for our reception of nonconventional bodies to say about the body's capacity to heal and enlarge our life together. It should be obvious to her now that, from where I sit, our current silent reception screams out that most biomedical, ecclesial and academic bodies are communicatively fractured and so restrictive that silence and surgery is the price of admission for some of us. This situation is unlikely to change until intersex and transgender people are no longer viewed as objects *of* care, but rather as full-fledged knowing and speaking subjects with something to say *about* their care. I am also convinced that Wesleyan intersex and transgender people have something to teach invariantly sex and cisgender people about caring for the atypically configured and marred body of Christ that continually feeds the hope of a whole and abundant life together.

BIBLIOGRAPHY

Ackley, H. Adam. "Transgender and Christian." Sermon originally presented at the Rector's Forum at All Saints Church, Pasadena, California, November 24, 2013. Revised version used by permission.

American Philosophical Association. "Gender Dysphoria." In *Diagnostic and Statistical Manual of Mental Disorders*, 5th ed., 451–59. Arlington, VA: American Psychiatric Publishing, 2012.

Arboleda, Valerie, and Eric Vilain. "Disorders of Sex Development." In *Yen & Jaffe's Reproductive Endocrinology: Physiology, Pathophysiology and Clinical Management*, edited by J. F. Strauss and R. Barbieri, 351–76. Philadelphia: Saunders, 2014.

Cornwall, Susannah. "Intersex Conditions (DSDs) and Pastoral Care: A Guide for Healthcare Chaplains, Ministers, and Pastoral Careers." Manchester, UK: Lincoln Theological Institute, 2012. http://religionandcivilsociety.com/iid-resources.

Ecklund, Kathryn "Intersectionality of Identity in Children: A Case Study." *Professional Psychology: Research and Practice* 43.3 (2012) 256–64. doi: 10.1037/a002865.

Eiesland, Nancy L. *The Disabled God: Toward a Liberatory Theology of Disability*. Nashville: Abingdon, 1994.

GLAAD. "An Ally's Guide to Terminology." http://www.glaad.org/sites/default/files/allys-guide-to-terminology_1.pdf.

Lee, Peter A., Christopher P. Houk, S. Faisal Ahmed, and Ieuan A. Hughes. "Consensus Statement on the Management of Intersex Disorders." *Pediatrics* 118 (2006) e488–e500. doi: 10.1542/peds.2006-0738.

Karkazis, Katrina. *Fixing Sex: Intersex, Medical Authority, and Lived Experience*. Durham: Duke University Press, 2008.

Morris, Sherrie G. "Twisted Lies: My Journey in an Imperfect Body." In *Surgically Shaping Children: Technology, Ethics and the Pursuit of Normality*, edited by Erik Parens, 3–12. Baltimore: The John Hopkins University Press, 2006.

Ngun, T. C., et al. "The Genetics of Sex Differences in Brain and Behavior." NIH Public Access: Author manuscript; available in PMC April 1, 2012. Published in final edited form as: *Front Neuroendocrinol* 32.2 (2011) 227–46. doi:10.1016/j.yfrne.2010.10.001.

Rametti, G., et al. "White Matter Microstructure in Female to Male Transsexuals before Cross-sex Hormonal Treatment. A Diffusion Tensor Imaging Study." *Journal of Psychiatric Research* 45.2 (2011) 199–204, doi: 10.1016/j.jpsychires.2010.05.006.

Sanders, C., B. Carter, and L. Goodacre. "Searching for Harmony: Parents' Narratives about Their Child's Genital Ambiguity and Reconstructive Genital Surgeries in Childhood." *Journal of Advanced Nursing* 67 (10) 2220–30. doi: 10.1111/j.1365-2648.2011.05617.x.

The United Kingdom Intersex Association. "Why Not 'Disorders of Sex Development.'" http://www.ukia.co.uk/ukia/dsd.html.

Williams, Rowan D. "The Body's Grace." In *Theology and Sexuality*, edited by Eugene F. Rogers Jr., 309–21. Oxford: Blackwell, 2002.

CHAPTER 10

A Mutilated Body
at (Intercessory) Prayer

Craig Keen

> If an artist were to paint a bloody wound admirably, the sight of
> the wound would strike me, but it would not be art.[1]

WE LOVE BEAUTY. INDEED, the love of beauty may be the most wholesome
and mainstream of all our loves. If I were standing delighted before an unambiguously beautiful event, the prolonged dancing of a flock of hundreds
of starlings sweeping coordinately in paisley patterns over a marsh on a
bright morning, say, all it would take for a confused passerby to understand my delight would be my gesturing toward the sky. There are beautiful sunsets, beautiful peach blossoms, beautiful gazelles, beautiful babies,
beautiful athletes, beautiful ballets, beautiful sculptures, beautiful theories,
beautiful arguments, beautiful minds, beautiful souls, beautiful obituaries.
No one has to be told that beauty is good. There are in fact undisputable
geniuses who would say that love is *always* in search of beauty, that if I love
something ugly, it is not the ugliness that I love, but the *beauty* that is still
vaguely visible behind an obscuring disfigurement, even if only to a mind

---

1. Tolstoy, *What is Art?*, 105.

that knows how to debride and suture a wound, how to restore the flood-damaged fresco of a master.

It is Plato above all who has taught us this in orthodox philosophical terms. The beautiful *is* the good, Plato tells us—and the beautiful is the good across our expansive gaze in a great, harmonized variety of ways—though in truth in just one way, itself seized upon by the sage who sagaciously assays the many.[2]

> For he who would proceed aright in this matter should begin in youth to visit beautiful forms; and, first, if he be guided by his instructor aright to love one such form only . . . a nature of wondrous beauty . . . a nature which in the first place is everlasting; not growing and decaying, or waxing and waning; secondly, not fair in one point of view [or at one time or in one relation or at one place] and foul in another, . . . but beauty absolute, separate, simple, and everlasting, which without diminution and without increase or any change is imparted to the ever-growing and perishing beauties of all other things.[3]

We love, you and I, as do in their own ways the starling, the gazelle, and the baby, but also the theory, the argument, and the obituary, all of which might also in one way or another serve us as signs on our love quest.[4] We all love and in loving we reach, however unconsciously, for the good that is good for us all and the happiness economically disbursed when the job of reaching it and into it is done. My chief task and yours is to reach for that *highest* good by reaching for the good both *derivative* from it and most *proper to* the human kind of being, your kind of being and mine. Other kinds of beings have other proper goods natural to them. This is your or my or their "entelechy," Aristotle tells us, the *telos* that is inherently good for my kind or your kind or their kind of entity.[5] When we look at an other and see that she or he or it has stumbled or fallen or succumbed in any other way

---

2. Plato, *Symposium*, 46 [205c–d].

3. Ibid., 51–52 [210a–212e].

4. Ibid., 48–50 [206e–209e].

5. Jaeger, *Paideia*, 20: According to Hippocrates, "Truth can never be dissolved into the infinite variety of individual cases; or, if it could, it would have no real meaning for us. That is how the medical thinkers of that age arrived at the conception of types (*eidē*) of human nature, of bodily structure, of dispositions, illnesses, and so forth. *Eidos* means, to begin with, 'form'; and then the visible 'signs' differentiating [forms] . . . ; but it is at once extended to any distinguishable features common to any multiplicity of related phenomena, and . . . takes the meaning of 'type' or 'kind.'"

to decompositional unruliness, whether by unwise decision or unfortunate accident, it is our task seriously to consider casting it away to its inevitable demise or, if it is not too late, if it is not too far gone from its authentic end, treating it with healing elixirs, i.e., to restore it, as physicians, to aid nature in *its* and thus *our* love for health.

Speaking this way is not casually analogical. Plato and Aristotle learned to imagine their peculiarly philosophical work from the medical theorists of their time and of the century just before. They pursue well-being not *like*, but *as* physicians, again, not merely rhetorically, but substantively.[6]

> Plato speaks of the three physical virtues—health, strength, and beauty—as joining to form one chorus with the virtues of the soul . . . . They all equally symbolize the symmetry of the world-order, the harmony which is reflected both in the physical and in the psychical life of the individual. Even physical culture, as understood by the Greek doctors and [gymnastic] trainers, . . . imposed one supreme standard upon men—the duty of preserving a noble and healthy balance between their physical powers. If, then, equality and harmony are the essence of health and all other physical perfections, then 'health' . . . grows into a universal standard of value applying to the whole world and to the whole of life . . . its foundations . . . the forces which . . . create that which is good and right . . . . Greek medical science was both the root and the fruit of this doctrine, from which it constantly draws strength and sustenance, and which . . . is the universal view of all classical Greeks.

6. Ibid., 24–27: "It is really astonishing to read the medical texts and discover how much they prefigure the method of 'Socrates' as described by Plato. . . . When the medical authors are speaking of a number of these types, they call them *eidē*; but when they want simply to bring out the unity underlying a complexity of phenomena, they use the concept of 'one Idea,' 'one Form'—i.e. one aspect or appearance (*mia idea*). . . . These concepts, first used by doctors in studying the body and its functions, were transferred by Plato to the . . . realm of ethics—and from there to his entire ontology. . . . It is important to realize that this principle [that every part supports and is supported by the others] in the development of Greek thought . . . is now confirmed in such a decisive point as the central Platonic and Aristotelian doctrine of human *aretē*. And it is not simply a matter of analogy, as it might seem at first glance. The medical doctrine of the correct treatment for the body is, so to speak, raised to a higher power when it is embodied in the Socratic doctrine of the correct care and treatment of the soul. Plato's and Aristotle's concept of the *aretē* of man contains the *aretai* of the body as well as those of the soul. . . . Greek medical thought was dominated by the idea of Nature [*physis*]. . . . Plato . . . wanted, by the example of medical method, to show that in every subject it is necessary to grasp the function of the part within the whole and thereby to define the appropriate treatment of the part. . . . So what he looked for without success in natural philosophy he found in medical science."

The reason why medicine rose to such a representative position in Greek culture was that it revealed, clearly and impressively . . . the inalienable significance of this fundamental Greek ideal. In this higher sense, we may say that the Greek ideal of culture was the ideal of Health.[7]

This "ideal of Health" did not fall with the fall of Athens, the rise of the Roman Empire, and the flourishing of Hellenism, or with their decline. Although Augustine is by no means an exemplary Roman or Hellenist and he stood among those whom the mainstream children of the *Pax Romana* regarded as threats to homeland security, he is among the most ardent advocates of wholeness, of health, of well being.

If we ask whence comes evil, we should first ask what evil is. It is nothing but the corruption of natural measure, form, or order. What is called an evil nature is a corrupt nature. If it were not corrupt it would be good. But even when it is corrupted, so far as it remains a natural thing, it is good. . . . All life, potency, health, memory, virtue, intelligence, tranquility, plenty, sense, light, sweetness, measure, beauty, peace—all these things . . . come from the Lord God.[8]

They come from the Lord God precisely because God the Creator is the wellspring of all perfections, in particular "the Good and the Beautiful, in, by and through whom all good and beautiful things have these qualities."[9] God makes beautiful things, nothing less than beautiful things. Certainly, some creatures are much more beautiful than others, but each has its own *proper* beauty. An ape may seem grotesque compared to a human being, but as an ape, as a creature at home in God's good synchronic and diachronic system of creatures, it is beautiful. Affliction—befalling an ape or any other being—is dis-integration of a creature's proper beauty, i.e., of its proper goodness, of its proper representation of divine beauty.[10]

You would think that, a millennium and a half later, we would have moved on from the ideals of bygone Greece and Rome, so much else has changed. However, we have not. If anything we are more transfixed than ever by what transfixed them. Their doctrine of well being above all keeps smooth as glass the surface of the vast sea in which we imagine we swim

7. Ibid., 45.

8. Augustine, "The Nature of the Good," 327, 329 [iv, xiii].

9. Augustine, "The Soliloquies," 24 [i, 3].

10. Augustine, "The Nature of the Good," 330 [xv].

and breathe. If asked what difference there might be between our conception of a comprehensively equilibrated nature, however constrained by the principles of physics or speculative ontology, and that of ancient Greek medical and philosophical theorists, a fair minded judge would be hard pressed to give a more appropriately coherent and wholesome answer than that they are variations on the same theme. Though they or we may appeal to the language of matter and form, potentiality and actuality, desire and satisfaction, replication and novelty, mass and energy, many and one, or some other tensile pair, i.e., in order to manage our troubles, it is hard for us to linger where no happy ending is in sight. We may think that the answer lies in the laws of thermodynamics or the great circle of life, but that something or someone might simply fall outside and thus rupture the integrity of it all, strikes us as unthinkable. We long ago yielded to the *theoria* and *praxis* of integrity so prevalent in Augustine and his Greek intellectual—especially medical—forebears. We think and imagine our humane and inhumane world—and us in it—as regimented by commanding therapeutic orders. Augustine is undoubtedly a theologian of grace and love. He hopes for the redemption of the world and believes that a merciful God heals those whom pervasive corrupting sin has diseased and disfigured, directly and indirectly. He could not countenance a world without paradise, a world forever undone, a world without the routing of "the inexplicable sufferings of small children, the horrors of the deformed and the mentally defective."[11] His desire is—as is ours—a future in which all broken things are mended, restored, whole and beautiful, once more the creatures they were created to be. And who could argue with him? Who would not long for universal restoration?

And yet . . . there she is, right before me, she from whom idealizing visions tempt me to avert my eyes, my love of beauty, as always, poised to

---

11. Betcher, *Spirit and the Politics of Disablement*, 206, n.1. She is quoting Brown, *Augustine of Hippo*, 396. Cf. Augustine, *City of God*, 1074–7 [22.24–25]: "For practical needs are, of course, transitory; and a time will come when we shall enjoy one another's beauty for itself alone, without any lust. . . . What will God give to those who are predestined to life, if he has given all these [beautiful earthly things] to those predestined for death? What blessings in that life of happiness will he provide for those for whom in this life of wretchedness he will that his only-begotten Son should endure such sufferings, even unto death? . . . How wonderful will be that body which will be completely subdued to the spirit, will receive from the spirit all that it needs for its life, and will need no other nourishment? It will not be animal; it will be a spiritual body, possessing the substance of flesh, but untainted by any carnal corruption. . . . There will be no corruption there, and corruption is the evil of the body."

filter her out, perhaps gently, turning in her direction with a prognostic teleological gaze, looking through her in a dream of higher, better possibilities, a future, say, rich, moist, bright, warm, and flourishing, however faintly simulacral such a dream may prove to have been once cooling tower updrafts die down and it drifts at last to the ground. "Disabled persons have often been, as Augustine makes clear, construed as the epitome of corruptibility—even as but a lump of matter without spirit. But where we still find disability serving as the physiognomic bottomlands, we might also then suspect reliance upon a metaphysical fantastic of nature itself."[12] It is precisely "a metaphysical fantastic of nature itself" that is the legacy of the ancient Greek physicians.

It is not enough to say that Western intellectual history has prioritized the non-corporeal over the corporeal. Its regard for the corporeal has itself prioritized not the bodies that we meet on the road, in the field, and at table, but an abstraction, an imaginary body, characterized by integrity, health, well being, authenticity, and totality, by measure, form, and order—by beauty. Thus they whose bodies are ravaged by injuries or deformities or diseases, by burns or gender anomalies or cancers, by beatings or congenital behavioral disorders or lupus, are customarily regarded quickly, from a distance, and on the way through, by Western intellectuals—by philosophers, theologians, physicians, and the other architects of a better tomorrow—as problems to be solved, as lacunae to be closed, as evils to be made good, as debts to be paid.

Strikingly large numbers of human beings never get over their afflictions, but live and die to one degree or another of debilitating agony, unfixed. Indeed, we all live and we all die unfixed, even the apparently beautiful people among us; we are all cut and broken to the end, persons without integrity, authenticity, or well being.

No one who has known and remembers heavy sorrow and loss has to strain to understand a prayer of lament or a prayer for healing. In spite of appearances, these are not simply the prayers of weak *ressentiment*. Strength and hope rise even in the most apparently desperate lament.

Hear my prayer, O Lord; let my cry come to you.

---

12. Ibid., 33. Cf. 45: "Ironically, since at least the time of Augustine, for Christianity, disabled bodies have been figural paradigms illustrating the extremes to which the Spirit must go to reclaim wholesomeness and, therefore, are indicative of the Holy Spirit's capacity for resurrecting life . . . that in a universe, pneumatically visited, resurrection names the remediatory normalization of [the disabled] body."

Do not hide your face from me in the day of my distress. Incline
your ear to me; answer me speedily in the day when I call.

For my days pass away like smoke, and my bones burn like a
furnace.

My heart is stricken and withered like grass; I am too wasted to
eat my bread.

Because of my loud groaning my bones cling to my skin.

I am like an owl of the wilderness, like a little owl of the waste
places.

I lie awake; I am like a lonely bird on the housetop.

All day long my enemies taunt me; those who deride me use my
name for a curse.

For I eat ashes like bread, and mingle tears with my drink,

because of your indignation and anger; for you have lifted me up
and thrown me aside.

My days are like an evening shadow; I wither away like grass.[13]

Yet what if another (perhaps renegade) prayer rose uncomely in some
inelegant moment—a prayer more awkward even than the most awkward
lament of a psalmist or of Job—an anarchic prayer prayed, perhaps verbally,
perhaps not, through tears, sweat, spit, blood, urine, and feces, idealizing
neither strength nor weakness, nobility nor ignobility, pleasure nor pain,
activity nor passivity, flourishing nor languishing—a freakish prayer, pray-
ing for the earthiest of all inarticulable shaloms?[14] Not lonely, private, or
isolated, it would pray "We!" even if by way of a shorter pronoun or none at
all—an intercessory prayer, not remembering perhaps in the weight of the
moment that I—whose throat would call out—am not alone (cf. 1 Kings
19). It would pray for no ordinary peace, exceeding or repulsing every
mainstream apparition of equilibrium, resolution, fulfillment, abundance—
a peace slipping beyond the grasp (*hyperechō*) of the understanding (Phil
4:7), a yearning "Here am I!" without proviso,[15] a prayer fueled otherwise

13. Ps 102:1–11

14. Seitz, "Prayer in the Old Testament," 16: "When one looks at prayer within the
covenant relationship, what is striking is what one does not find. There is no handbook
on prayer, as there is on sacrifice and offerings. The elaborate details that governed Israel's worship have not a single specific word about how to pray or what to pray for. Here
again one is thrown up against the reality that prayer in the Old Testament is distinctly
nonreligious. Spirituality is religious, phenomenal, and self-conscious. But prayer in the
Old Testament lacks the dimension of self-consciousness."

15. Cf. *Oxford English Dictionary*, s.v. "proviso, *conj.* and *n.1*": "< post-classical Latin

than with the autoimmune desire of cycles of abuse: "Abba, Father, for you all things are possible; remove this cup from me!" "Yet, not what I want, but what you want!" "My God, my God, why have you forsaken me?" "Father, into your hands I commend my spirit." It would be a prayer that steps into an impossible future whispering "we do not live to ourselves, and we do not die to ourselves," but that "if we live, we live . . . , and if we die, we die . . ." to an *other*, an *alien*, an inappropriable *outside*, an unspeakable *moronism* and *superfluity*, that "whether we live or whether we die" . . . we are not held fast by a "what is" or a "what was" or an extrapolative "what will be," but open, as a bloody wound, to a "what is to come" that rips through every integrity, wholeness, health, well being, authenticity, and totality, every measure, form, and order, every beauty. This would be a vagabond prayer calling out in the dust of a dusty road for an outlandish unmending of the mutilated good, true, and beautiful body of late night Western fantasy, a prayer that would mark us freakishly, you or me, as "that one." It would be a prayer by which the anomalous would yearn for a future dis-integration, a yearning that would abide not vis-à-vis an assured identity, but hopefully after an unforeclosable glory, peace, and freedom, i.e., a love that would not need satiety, an atonement that would not need a receipt.

---

proviso (in formula *proviso quod* (legal phrase) it being provided that"; s.v. "proviso, *n.2*": "Apparently < Italian regional (Venice) *provese* (a1487), probably ultimately < post-classical Latin *prosnesium* mooring rope . . . ."

BIBLIOGRAPHY

Augustine. *Concerning the City of God Against the Pagans.* Translated by Henry Bettenson. Edited by David Knowles. New York: Penguin, 1972.

———. *The Nature of the Good Against the Manichees.* In *Augustine: Earlier Writings,* translated by John H. S. Burleigh, 326–48. Philadelphia: Westminster, 1953.

———. *The Soliloquies.* In *Augustine: Earlier Writings,* translated by John H. S. Burleigh, 23–63. Philadelphia: Westminster, 1953.

Betcher, Sharon V. *Spirit and the Politics of Disablement.* Minneapolis: Fortress, 2007.

Brown, Peter. *Augustine of Hippo: A Biography.* Berkeley: University of California Press, 1967.

Jaeger, Werner. *Paideia: The Ideals of Greek Culture.* Volume 3, *The Conflict of Cultural Ideals in the Age of Plato.* Translated by Gilbert Highet. New York: Oxford University Press, 1971.

Plato. *Symposium.* Tranlated by Benjamin Jowett. Indianapolis: Bobbs-Merrill Educational, 1956.

Seitz, Christopher. "Prayer in the Old Testament or Hebrew Bible." In *God's Presence: Prayer in the New Testament,* edited by Richard N. Longenecker, 3–22. Grand Rapids: Eerdmans, 2002.

Tolstoy, Leo N. *What Is Art?* Translated by Almyer Maude. Indianapolis: Bobbs-Merrill, 1960.

Index

Index

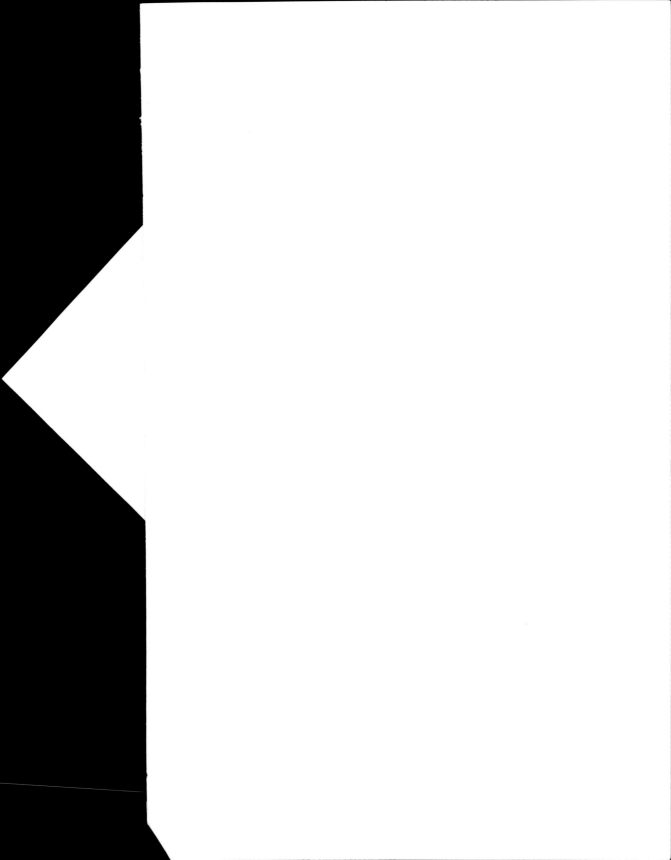

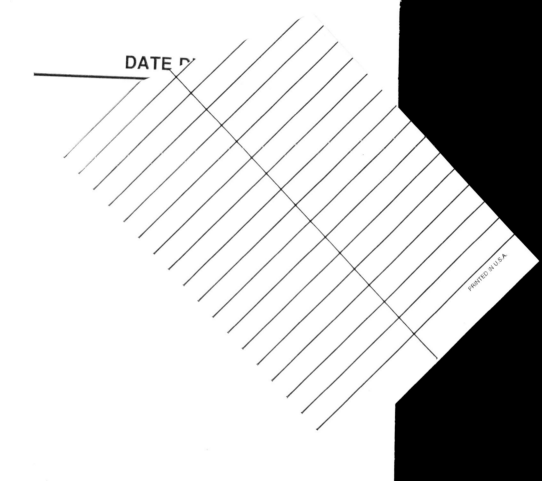

DATE D

PRINTED IN U.S.A.

Made in the USA
Lexington, KY
20 March 2016